D0840544

Feminist Theory & Simone de Beauvoir

THE BUCKNELL LECTURES IN LITERARY THEORY
General Editors: Michael Payne and Harold Schweizer

The lectures in this series explore some of the fundamental changes in literary studies that have occurred during the past thirty years in response to new work in feminism, Marxism, psychoanalysis, and deconstruction. They assess the impact of these changes and examine specific texts in the light of this new work. Each volume in the series includes a critical assessment of the lecturer's own publications, an interview, and a comprehensive bibliograpy.

Frank Kermode   *Poetry, Narrative, History*
Terry Eagleton   *The Significance of Theory*
Toril Moi   *Feminist Theory and Simone de Beauvoir*

Feminist Theory & Simone de Beauvoir

Toril Moi

Basil Blackwell

Copyright © Toril Moi 1990
Introductory and editorial matter copyright © Michael Payne and
Laura Payne 1990
First published 1990

Basil Blackwell Ltd
108 Cowley Road, Oxford, OX4 1JF, UK

Basil Blackwell, Inc.
3 Cambridge Center
Cambridge, Massachusetts 02142, USA

All rights reserved. Except for the quotation of short passages for the
purposes of criticism and review, no part of this publication may be
reproduced, stored in a retrieval system, or transmitted, in any form
or by any means, electronic, mechanical, photocopying, recording or
otherwise, without the prior permission of the publisher.

Except in the United States of America, this book is sold subject to
the condition that it shall not, by way of trade or otherwise, be lent,
re-sold, hired out, or otherwise circulated without the publisher's
prior consent in any form of binding or cover other than that in
which it is published and without a similiar condition including this
condition being imposed on the subsequent purchaser.

British Library Cataloguing in Publication Data

A CIP catalogue record for this book is available from the British
Library.

Library of Congress Cataloging in Publication Data

Moi, Toril.
    Feminist theory and Simone de Beauvoir/Toril Moi.
        p. cm. — (The Bucknell lectures in literary theory)
    Includes bibliographical references.
    ISBN 0–631–17323–4 — ISBN 0–631–17324–2 (pbk.)
    1. Beauvoir, Simone de. 1908– —Criticism and interpretation-
-History. 2. Beauvoir, Simone de. 1908– —Political and social
views. 3. Feminism and literature—France. 4. Feminist literary
criticism. I. Title. II. Series.
PQ2603.E362785 1989   89–38729
848′.91409—dc20   CIP

Typeset in 11 on 13pt Plantin
by Photographics, Honiton, Devon
Printed in Great Britain by Billing & Sons Ltd, Worcester

Contents

Preface

Fundamental and far-reaching changes in literary studies, often compared to paradigmatic shifts in the sciences, have been taking place during the last thirty years. These changes have included enlarging the literary canon not only to include novels, poems and plays by writers whose race, gender or nationality had marginalized their work but also to include texts by philosophers, psychoanalysts, historians, anthropologists, social and religious thinkers, who previously were studied by critics merely as 'background'. The stance of the critic and student of literature is also now more in question than ever before. In 1951 it was possible for Cleanth Brooks to declare with confidence that the critic's job was to describe and evaluate literary objects, implying the relevance for criticism of the model of scientific objectivity while leaving unasked questions concerning significant issues in scientific theory, such as complementarity, indeterminacy and the use of metaphor. Now the possibility of value-free scepticism is itself in doubt as many feminist, Marxist and psychoanalytic theorists have stressed the inescapability of ideology and the consequent obligation of teachers and students of literature to declare their political, axiological and aesthetic positions in order to make those positions conscious and available for examination. Such expansion and deepening of literary studies has, for many critics, revitalized their field.

Those for whom the theoretical revolution has been regenerative would readily echo, and apply to criticism, Lacan's call to revitalize psychoanalysis: 'I consider it to be an urgent task to disengage from concepts that are being deadened by routine use the meaning that they regain both from a re-examination of their history and from a reflexion on their subjective foundations. That, no doubt, is the teacher's prime function.'

Many practising writers and teachers of literature, however, see recent developments in literary theory as dangerous and anti-humanistic. They would insist that displacement of the centrality of the word, claims for the 'death of the author', emphasis upon gaps and incapacities in language, and indiscriminate opening of the canon threaten to marginalize literature itself. In this view the advance of theory is possible only because of literature's retreat in the face of aggressive moves by Marxism, feminism, deconstruction and psychoanalysis. Furthermore, at a time of militant conservativism and the dominance of corporate values in America and Western Europe, literary theory threatens to diminish further the declining audience for literature and criticism. Theoretical books are difficult to read; they usually assume that their readers possess knowledge that few have who have received a traditional literary education; they often require massive reassessments of language, meaning and the world; they seem to draw their life from suspect branches of other disciplines: professional philosophers usually avoid Derrida; psychoanalysts dismiss Freud as unscientific; Lacan was excommunicated even by the International Psycho-Analytical Association.

The volumes in this series record part of the attempt at Bucknell University to sustain conversation about changes in literary studies, the impact of those changes on literary art and the significance of literary theory for the humanities and human sciences. A generous grant from the Andrew W. Mellon Foundation has made possible a five-year series of visiting lectureships by internationally known participants in the reshaping of literary studies. Each volume includes a comprehensive introduction to the published work of the lecturer, the two Bucknell Lectures, an interview and a comprehensive bibliography.

For Terry

Introduction

During the past thirty years, the theoretical work of feminists, Marxists, psychoanalysts and post-modernists has made it impossible to ignore that all discourse is ideologically situated and that meaning manifests itself by endless processes of deferral, displacement and revision. The shape and body of the time in which we live, to recall Hamlet's words to the Players, exert pressure upon us and assume forms moulded by our lived experience. Rather than being able to choose to be removed from that pressure, we can instead choose to make ourselves conscious of its impact and in turn can determine whether to accept the shape of our time as it comes to us or to resist and struggle to reshape it.

Sexism has generated political, moral, and intellectual pressure that cannot be ignored. That women have been systematically oppressed by patriarchy for millenia is inescapably obvious now to any student of the humanities and human sciences. Evidence of rare, enlightened dissent in the past from such patriarchal practice simply reveals that ubiquitous sexism was not necessarily innocent or simply unconscious. Feminism now calls with articulate passion for the end of patriarchy; and feminist literary theory brings the insights of post-modernism, psychoanalysis and Marxism to that political project. Since all discourse is situated and since ours is a time of the continuing oppression of patriarchy, each child who is initiated into language is simultaneously initiated into sexism. Language is already political before we learn to speak; literature already ideological before we read.

Many women have become so embittered by their own specific experiences of patriarchal oppression that they want feminism to be an exclusively female project. There is an active tradition within feminism, however, that cautiously but generously welcomes men. Mary Wollstonecraft, Virginia Woolf, Simone de Beauvoir, Julia Kristeva, Toril Moi have all envisioned 'men and women working together for the same cause' (Woolf, *Three Guineas* (London, 1938) p. 185), recognizing especially the need to appropriate by revision the work of men for feminism. 'We can only destroy the mythical and mystifying constructions of patriarchy by using its own weapons. We have no others', Moi insists, (*RP*, p. 198). The dangers of well-intentioned participation but ignorant betrayal of feminism by men are manifold, however. Even to praise the work of a feminist woman is an inescapably situated act. To claim that Toril Moi's work displays a powerful, lucid and articulate intelligence that affirms art while exposing its political dimension invites the suspicion of praising her work because of her systematic criticism of the best books and articles by feminists since Simone de Beauvoir's *The Second Sex* (1949). The counter-argument that Moi's task is to help feminist literary theory refine itself in order to become the best of current theoretical projects and best able to achieve its political ends can simply put the earlier suspicion 'under erasure'; it cannot obliterate it. Even as knowledgeable and otherwise politically sensitive a commentator as K. K. Ruthven, in the first survey of feminist literary studies, has put himself in the untenable position of implying that feminism is too important to be left to women and that there are feminist jobs that had better be left to men. Training of the male feminist voice has just begun.

Even though men have no reason to assume that women feminists should assign a high priority to initiating males properly into feminism, the risks of error from autodidacticism are worth taking, perhaps inevitably must be taken if for no other reason than to avoid the reappearance of sexism within feminism itself. At the present time men who teach literature in Europe and America typically teach far more female than male students. (In America this situation is intensified by an even higher proportion of women to men among racial minorities who study literature.) How these students are to be initiated into literary theory is a pressing question at a time when the patriarchalism of traditional discourse is being made manifest, when traditional definitions of 'literature' have become thoroughly suspect and when literary theory in all its forms insists on the self-reflexivity of reading and of criticism. Furthermore, what begins as a parochial matter of pedagogy expands far beyond the classroom and academic politics once literature, criticism and theory are seriously taken as being about the encounter of readers with all forms of situated discourse, or, even more broadly, about initiation into a language intricately marked by culture. The teacher's identity as scholar, parent, lover, political activist is always at issue whenever he or she engages students in conversation over a text. The attempt to suspend convictions about feminism in such encounters is simply to leave those convictions – whatever they may be – unmarked and unavailable for discussion and criticism.

Toril Moi's work manifests a set of well-marked, closely related convictions. Feminism, she argues, is a political project dedicated to 'the struggle against patriarchy and sexism' and is, therefore, distinguishable from 'femaleness' – 'a matter of biology' – and 'femininity' – 'a set of culturally defined characteristics' (*MP*, p. 152). As a political movement, feminism requires a sense of its own history, which Moi sees as unfolding in three cumulative phases, corresponding to the generations of European feminism outlined by Julia Kristeva in her famous essay 'Women's Time': (1) the demand for 'equal access to the symbolic order'; (2) the rejection of 'the male symbolic order in the name of difference'; and (3) the rejection of 'the dichotomy between masculine and feminine as metaphysical' (see *STP*, p. 12). In England, stage one may be said to date from Mary Wollstonecroft, though F. M. Cornford, in his edition of Plato's *Republic*, cites Aristophanes' *Ecclesiazusae (Women in Parliament)* and the section on the equality of women in the *Republic* (IV.445B–V.457B) to show that 'the question of women's rights was in the air as early as 393 BC' (*The Republic of Plato* (Oxford, 1941) p. 141). Kristeva dates stage two from the uprisings in Paris of 1968 and launches the argument for stage three herself in 1979. Although Kristeva and Moi stress the importance of stage three as a check against the inverted sexism of what Kristeva calls a second sex 'counter-society' (*KR*, p. 202), the coming into being of the third generation implies the parallel existence, or the interweaving, of the earlier stages with it. Kristeva suggests that the use of her word 'generation' might be thought of as implying 'less a chronology than a *signifying space*' (*KR*, p. 209).

To deconstruct effectively the dichotomy between masculine and feminine in order to expose that dichotomy as perversely metaphysical and erroneously essentialist requires all the theoretical subtlety and intellectual power that can be critically appropriated from Derrida and Lacan. If truly committed to eliminating patriarchy, feminism must be prepared to meet its own determined end and to move on to other political issues: 'if true postfeminism presupposes postpatriarchy, only a feminist can be a postfeminist' (*FPS*, p. 13). Although in her current work Moi calls for a recovery of Simone de Beauvoir, just as she argued for feminists' overcoming their fears of Woolf, she carefully distances herself none the less from Beauvoir's rejection of psychoanalysis and from her substitution of

Sartrian existentialism for traditional Marxism. Although she calls Beauvoir 'the greatest feminist theorist of our time' (*STP*, p. 91), Moi supplements *The Second Sex* by finding in the Marxist tradition of literary criticism a model for revealing the gaps and ideological determinants of texts, which can both contribute to the achievement of feminism's immediate goals and continue to be of use in achieving the goals of socialism.

Moi's politically confrontational view of feminism, her outline of its history, her adaptations of deconstruction and psychoanalysis, and her Marxism are all powerfully active in the argument of *Sexual/Textual Politics* (1985). Moi begins her book by asking why so many feminist critics would seem to be afraid of Virgina Woolf, arguably the most important feminist writer in English of this century. Rather than offering a reading of Woolf, Moi examines instead 'the relationship between feminist critical readings and the often unconscious theoretical and political assumptions that inform them' (*STP*, p. 1), focusing her critique on Elaine Showalter. In *A Literature of Their Own* Showalter argues that although Woolf expresses feminist conflicts, she erroneously wants to transcend them. Thus, Woolf's emphasis falls on the androgynous nature of the great writer in flight from feminism. Furthermore, in Showalter's view, Woolf's narrative strategy – that is, her art – denies an authentic feminist state of mind, revealing instead her commitment to the Bloomsbury ideal of the separation of politics from art.

In rebuttal Moi argues, however, that Showalter's views of Woolf reveal Showalter's own preference for bourgeois realism over modernism, for works that attempt directly to mirror society rather than for those that suggest the problems of how we see and think and write about the world. Showalter's quarrel with Woolf, then, is an aesthetic one, not simply a feminist one. Like Lukács, Showalter would prefer to see in fiction a didactic demonstration of how inhuman social conditions frustrate the development of the whole person. But this assumes, Moi points out, the notion of a unitary self as the basic reality. Such an assumption has produced the very circumstances Showalter is reacting against. Woolf, in Moi's view, calls into question the humanist ideology of the self, the conception of the creator as 'potent, phallic, and male' (*STP*, p. 8). While reclaiming her for feminist politics, Moi insists that Woolf practises deconstructive writing by engaging and exposing the duplicitous nature of discourse and the refusal of language to be pinned down to a single meaning. Behind Woolf's view of language is her critique of the assumption of an essential, unitary self, which is the very conception to which Showalter clings. The quest for single meanings, for a unified self, for fixed gender definitions is (for Woolf and for Moi) reductive and false.

In these matters Woolf has anticipated, according to Moi, the thinking of Julia Kristeva. For Kristeva such views as Woolf's concerning language, self and gender have important revolutionary social implications, including 'the possibility of transforming the symbolic order of orthodox society from the inside' (*STP*, p. 11). Such disruption of the symbolic order runs the risk, Moi admits, of madness; indeed, Moi observes that Woolf's own attacks of madness can be linked to her textual strategies and her feminism. Moi concludes her critique of feminist readings of Woolf with an affirmation of her art and politics: Woolf 'has understood that the goal of the feminist struggle must precisely be to deconstruct the death-dealing binary oppositions of masculinity and femininity' (*STP*, p. 13). Furthermore, Woolf may have succeeded better than Kristeva in dealing also with the material (economic) forces that oppress women. Finally, the politics of Woolf's writing can be found in her textual practice – in how she says what she says – and does not necessarily require the reactionary biographical critical methods of Elaine Showalter or Jane Marcus.

This opening chapter of *Sexual/Textual Politics* displays

many of Moi's most outstanding qualities as a feminist literary theorist. She assumes feminist studies to be a mature discipline that can withstand and benefit from a critique of itself, like all mature disciplines. She demonstrates the need to be fully responsive to the subtleties of discourse, both literary and critical. She knows that women are subject to the same limited horizons of understanding and unconscious psychological and political processes as men. She is optimistic about the advance of feminist studies, which she sees (along with Woolf, Beauvoir and Kristeva) as conceptually evolving and moving toward the attainment of its political objectives. She reads feminist theoretical books as texts that invite the kinds of critique they themselves perform on other texts. She recognizes the limits of 'narcissistic' autobiography and consequently the limits of biographical criticism. She argues convincingly that feminist criticism begins with a deconstruction of an assumed opposition between the political and the aesthetic. And she seeks to promote the relationship between feminism and Marxism, which has been virtually absent in American feminist literary criticism.

Sexual/Textual Politics does not simply oppose sophisticated French theoretical feminism to naïve Anglo-American critical method; rather, its purpose is to stimulate debate within feminism in order to achieve the principal objective of feminist criticism, which is 'to expose, not to perpetuate, patriarchal practices' (*STP*, p. xiv). Moi carefully demonstrates that such practices are not specific to male critics. Politically committed women feminists often undermine their own convictions by unintentionally doing what they deplore in work by men. Theoretical self-awareness is perhaps the only effective safeguard against political and aesthetic interests short-circuiting each other. Moi's book, therefore, invites being read as two arguments in one, each argument unfolding in two parts. The first argument is a narrative account and critique of feminist criticism in English – from Kate Millett to Myra Jehlen (part I) – and in French – from Simone de Beauvoir to Julia Kristeva (part II). This apparently negative argument can be read also against the grain of its sequential argument in order to discover the book's own affirmations. Once these affirmations surface, as they repeatedly do, especially in part II, they in turn invite the application of the same techniques of scrutiny that Moi uses in her examination of other feminist writers. Unlike most of the critics she discusses, however, Moi encourages her readers to recognize her affirmations and to debate them with her. 'The difference between feminist and non-feminist criticism', she argues, 'is not . . . that the former is political and the latter is not, but that the feminist openly declares her politics, whereas the non-feminist may either be unaware of his own value-system or seek to universalize it as "non-political"' (*STP*, p. 84).

While repeatedly praising Anglo-American feminists for their political engagement, Moi systematically exposes the weaknesses in the work of those thinkers she otherwise admires. She finds Kate Millett deficient because in her *Sexual Politics* (1977) she deals exclusively with male writers, misreads and misunderstands Freud, and bases her critical readings and cultural analysis on a 'monolithic conception of sexual ideology' (*STP*, p. 30). Although they champion the work of women writers, the essayists represented in Susan Koppelman Cornillon's *Images of Women in Fiction* (1972) display an unexamined bias (like Showalter's) in favour of realism and against modernism in fiction, which is inconsistent with their simultaneous demand for positive role models for women readers. Ellen Moers's *Literary Women* (1976) is 'too engrossed in circumstantial details, too unaware of any kind of literary theory to function well as criticism, and far too limited in its conception of history and its relations to literature to be convincing as historiography' (*STP*, p. 54). Sandra Gilbert and Susan Gubar, on the other hand, in *The Madwoman in the Attic* (1979), insist on the eventual identity of author and character, reduce the truth or meaning of women's texts to 'constant, never-changing *feminist rage*' (*STP*, p. 62), practice patriarchal criticism unwittingly themselves by relying on 'the author as the transcendental signified of his or her text' (*STP*, p. 62), refuse 'to admit a separation between nature and nurture at the lexical level' (*STP*, p. 65) of discourse by not distinguishing femaleness from femininity and feminism, and continue to labour under the patriarchal aesthetic values of unity and wholeness espoused by the New Critics. Although more theoretically sophisticated than Gilbert and Gubar, Annette Kolodny argues for a separation of political ideology from aesthetic judgement, rejects psychoanalysis and Marxism in the name of pluralism, and fails to recognize the role of politics in critical theory. Elaine Showalter, in *A Literature of Their Own* (1977), mistakenly reserves the hermeneutics of suspicion for works by male writers as though all women writers were feminists, rejects theory as a male project, recognizes only extra-literary cultural influences as constituting a text, and manifests a humanist ideology in her critical practice that amounts to complicity with the male academic hierarchy she wants to resist. Myra Jehlen errs in thinking of ideological criticism as reductive, rather than as methodology that declares its politics, and thus comes to accept traditional patriarchal aesthetic categories in a way that is 'astonishing in a critic who calls herself a feminist' (*STP*, p. 82).

As she proceeds with her candid examination of feminist criticism, Moi allows her own positive argument to rise to the surface. She affirms Kate Millett's rejection of the image of the 'reader/critic as passive/feminine recipient of *autho*ritarian discourse' (*STP*, p. 25), which leads her in turn to praise Mary Ellmann's use of irony and satire in *Thinking About Women* (1968), claiming, in opposition to Millett, that 'anger is not the only revolutionary attitude available to us' (*STP*, p. 40). Although Moi readily admits that there are limits to how clearly writers can state their own positions – ('we cannot fully grasp our own "horizon of understanding"' (*STP*, p. 44) – she nevertheless lays the foundation for a theoretically enlightened and politically effective feminist criticism. For feminism to explore and eliminate patriarchy, it must know what it is working against: 'Patriarchal oppression consists of imposing certain social standards of femininity on all biological women, in order precisely to make us believe that the chosen standards for "femininity" are *natural*' (*STP*, p. 65). But in order for feminists to oppose patriarchy while working as literary critics, they must overcome the common contradiction in Anglo-American feminist criticism between politics and aesthetics. That literature is politically encoded not only means that there is work to be done by feminists in making literature's politics conscious; it also means that one's perception of the formal aesthetics of literature may determine if or how one is able to expose the ideology of texts. Feminist criticism, therefore, 'is about deconstructing . . . an opposition between the political and the aesthetic: as a political approach to criticism, feminism must be aware of the politics of aesthetic categories as well as of the implied aesthetics of political approaches to art' (*STP*, p. 86). Finally, Moi insists, feminists must recognize the politics of their own theories no less than the politics of literature. In order to become fully political, American feminist criticism needs to free itself from those critical theories – such as organic unity, the wholeness of the self, authorial determination of meaning – that perpetuate patriarchal practice in literary studies. Feminism is determined to eradicate all such practice in any form of knowledge or action in which it appears.

The method of part II of *Sexual/Textual Politics* shifts significantly from that of part I, resulting in a change in tone that has invited some readers to misconstrue the entire book as simply promoting French feminist theory at the expense of Anglo-American feminist criticism. Always engaged in the effort to stimulate open and productive debate within feminism, however, Moi assumes throughout her book that her English-speaking readers will be better acquainted with the authors in part I than they are with those in part II; thus, she devotes more space to detailed summary of the thought of Hélène Cixous, Luce Irigaray and Julia Kristeva than she did to the work of the Anglo-American feminists of part I. The French theorists are not spared Moi's suspecting glance. Although she wants to help secure a wider Anglo-American audience for French feminists, Moi readily admits that they have done little to create that audience themselves:

> One of the reasons for the relatively limited influence of French theory on Anglo-American feminists is the 'heavy' intellectual profile of the former. Steeped as they are in European philosophy (particularly Marx, Nietzsche and Heidegger), Derridean deconstruction and Lacanian psychoanalysis, French feminist theorists apparently take for granted an audience as Parisian as they are. (*STP*, p. 96)

In addition to its intellectual difficulty, the work of French feminists may not at first appear to Anglo-American readers to be literary criticism at all because of relative indifference to disciplinary boundaries. Like Beauvoir, Lacan and Derrida, contemporary French feminist critics have focused their attention on problems that are broadly textual, philosophical, psychoanalytic, linguistic or semiotic. Their willingness to cross arbitrary academic barriers, however, poses a major challenge and offers a powerful example both to the feminism and to the literary criticism of Anglo-Americans. Like Lacan, who insists that psychoanalysis must continually revitalize itself by examining its own assumptions and techniques, Moi confronts her British and American readers with fundamental challenges to feminist theory and practice.

Hélène Cixous offers so radical a challenge to feminism

as to have declared that she is not a feminist at all. Moi explains that Cixous avoids the feminist label because she sees many in the women's movement as simply issuing 'a bourgeois, egalitarian demand for women to obtain power in the present patriarchal system' (*STP*, p. 103). Nevertheless, because of her committment to women's liberation and her critique of patriarchal thought, Moi argues, Cixous is clearly a feminist. Although she sets out to deconstruct the logocentric ideology that underlies the opposition man/woman by advocating heterogeneous diffference, feminine writing, and 'other bisexuality', Cixous herself simply creates other binary oppositions and an alternative metaphysics. Furthermore, Moi observes, Cixous's creation of a utopian poetic mythology leads her to neglect the material factors that have perpetuated the inequalities that women suffer. Luce Irigaray's work also fails, in Moi's judgement, adequately to consider 'the historical and economic specificity of patriarchal power' (*STP*, p. 148). But her strength as a thinker and her effective mimicry of phallocentric thought are both mirrored in Moi's critique, especially in such passages as these:

> If our theorist were to think the feminine, he might find himself tumbling from his phallic lighthouse into the obscurity of the dark continent.   (*STP*, p. 134)

> The blindspot of the master thinker's discourse is always woman: exiled from representation, she constitutes the ground on which the theorist erects his specular constructs, but she is therefore also always the point on which his erections subside.   (*STP*, p. 136)

What Moi seems most to admire in Irigaray are her critical virtuosity, her subtle intelligence and her intellectual range. Irigaray's incisive critiques of Plato, Plotinus, Descartes, Kant, Hegel, Nietzsche, Freud and Heidegger continue to send shock waves through feminism and psychoanalysis.

Because of her adoption early in her book of Julia Kristeva's outline of feminism's history, Moi leads her reader to expect a general affirmation of Kristeva in her final chapter. Instead, Moi's method of double argument from part I joins forces here with the technique of critical summary employed throughout part II. Rather than deriving her theoretical and political stance from Kristeva, Moi works first with and then beyond Kristevan thought. Both Kristeva and Moi are *étrangères*: Kristeva, a Bulgarian living in Paris; Moi, a Norwegian living in Britain and writing in English about French feminist theory in part for an American audience. Moi affirms Kristeva's linguistic emphasis on the speaking subject, developed out of the thought of Marx, Freud and Nietzsche, not only because that emphasis allows her to understand language as a process rather than as a monolithic system, but also because it has important significance for feminism. Like the Soviet linguist Vološinov, however, Kristeva finds it necessary to transcend the barrier of the sentence, which has defined the field of structural linguistics, in order to examine whole compositional forms. Once the barriers separating linguistics, rhetoric and poetics are deconstructed, semiotics emerges to study intertextuality. Because all meaning is contextually determined, language is not itself sexist, feminist or patriarchal: 'the question of sexism is a question of the power relationship between the sexes, and this power struggle will of course be part of the *context* of all utterance under patriarchy' (*STP*, p. 157). Despite her early commitment to Marxism, as well as her idealization of Maoism in the 1970s, Kristeva has withdrawn from political engagement to pursue her primary interests in individuals. This leads Moi to observe that Kristeva 'is unable to account for the relations between the subject and society' and 'conveniently chooses to overlook the differences between the "dissident" groups she enumerates: the rebel (who attacks political power), the psychoanalyst, the *avant-garde* writer and women' (*STP*, p. 171). Kristeva admirably succeeds, however, in Moi's view, in carrying out a thorough theoretical investigation of marginality and subversion and in developing a theory of language capable of examining writing by men and women in a way that avoids the pitfalls of essentialism. Moi further suggests that Kristeva's vision, when applied to problems of sexual identity and difference, 'becomes a feminist vision of a society in which the sexual signifier would be free to move; where the fact of being born male or female no longer would determine the subject's position in relation to power, and where, therefore, the very nature of power itself would be transformed' (*STP*, p. 172).

Moi's project of introducing new French feminist thought to an English-speaking audience is continued in her acclaimed but controversial anthologies: *The Kristeva Reader* (1986) and *French Feminist Thought* (1987). The first collection stresses Kristeva's difference, not only as a young Bulgarian woman entering the French intellectual scene in 1966, but also as a foreign and subversive voice even within the new, challenging science of semiotics. In her introduction, Moi traces the double heritage of Kristeva. From Bakhtin's dialogism, Kristeva develops her emphasis on the speaking subject and her concept of intertextuality; and from Hegel and Marx, she appropriates the concepts of negativity, alienation and marginality. When she visited China with the *Tel Quel* group in 1974, however, Kristeva found her past experiences under East European communism coming together with her observation of the oppression of women in Maoist China:

What I saw was very problematic, particularly in the situation of women. . . . And personally from the point of view of my own development I thought that it would be more honest for me not to engage politically but to try to be helpful or useful in a narrow field, where the individual life is concerned. (*KR*, p. 7)

Moi points out that Kristeva's work since her China trip and her subsequent training in psychoanalysis has been less political, and she has bluntly criticized feminists who would politicize all human relationships.

French Feminist Thought seeks to represent the diversity of French feminism in the seventies and eighties. Although the voices of Beauvoir, Kristeva and Irigaray are briefly heard in this book, its main emphasis is on the work of women whose feminism developed within the revolutionary political/intellectual context of Paris 1968 and its aftermath. Moi concludes her introduction to this anthology by insisting that her book is designed to challenge the view that it is simply an exercise in nostalgia to look back on French feminist thought when feminism is already in some ways advancing into post-feminism. Here she again celebrates the theoretical self-criticism of the best feminist research and argues the necessity of feminism's situating itself in opposition to patriarchal power.

The relationship between Moi's advocacy of theoretical self-criticism (the basis of her epistemology) and her strategic feminism (the principal direction of her politics) is carefully developed in a sequence of important papers published since 1981. 'Representation of Patriarchy: Sexuality and Epistemology in Freud's Dora' (1981) begins with a brief review of feminist critiques of Freud's 'Fragment of an Analysis of a Case of Hysteria', showing that the common feminist conclusion has been that 'Freud's analysis fails because of its inherent sexism' (*RP*, p. 182). This judgement has often led feminists to dismiss Freud and psychoanalysis completely and to elevate Dora to the position of 'a radiant example of feminine revolt' (*RP*, p. 192) because she terminated Freud's attempt to become her psychoanalytic liberator. Moi rejects these polemical moves, as well as depoliticized readings of Freud's text: 'Feminists', she insists, 'must neither reject theoretical discussion as "beyond feminist polemics" nor forget the ideological context of theory' (*RP*, p. 184). She then proceeds to turn Freud's own analytical procedure back on his text. Freud's obsession with the fragmentary condition of his text, the abrupt termination of his analysis, his incomplete knowledge of Dora's condition, his reluctant recognition that all psychoanalytic knowledge is incomplete lead Moi to see a double conflict manifested in Freud's paper: (1) On the one hand, Freud honestly admits the limitations of what he knows, what Dora has let him know and what he has been able to piece together; on the other hand, he wants complete knowledge, mastery of Dora, mythic power as an analyst. (2) But this conflict in Freud's epistemology, Moi shows, is intimately related to his patriarchal ideology, which prevents him from understanding Dora, mars his theory of 'feminine' sexuality and keeps him from explicitly revealing his own hysteria and castration fears. Freud conceals his psychoanalytic technique precisely because his epistemology is so interwoven with his patriarchal ideology. 'The penis, in other words, becomes the epistemological object par excellence for Freud' (*RP*, p. 196), which he can almost bring himself to admit in his account of Little Hans but which he attempts to conceal in his account of Dora. Moi concludes her superb analysis of Freud by exposing the untenable foundation of his epistemology:

> Nowhere is patriarchal ideology to be seen more clearly than in the definition of the feminine as the negative of the masculine – and this is precisely how Freud defines Dora and the 'feminine' epistemiology she is supposed to represent.
>   To undermine this phallocentric epistemology means to expose its lack of 'natural' foundation. In the case of *Dora*, however, we have been able to do this only because of Freud's own theories of femininity and sexuality. The attack upon phallocentrism must come from within, since

there can be no 'outside', no space where true femininity, untainted by patriarchy, can be kept intact for us to discover. We can only destroy the mythical and mystifying constructions of patriarchy by using its own weapons. We have no others. (*RP*, p. 198)

Freud is a necessary appropriation for feminism precisely because he provides the means to attack phallocentrism from within, just as Moi has done, both here and in all of her work. By 'mastering' the methods of 'masculine' critique, Moi has appropriated psychoanalysis and Derridean deconstruction for feminism while unmasking the illusion that epistemological methods can be divided into masculine and feminine categories. Freud's longing for completeness and mastery is a pathological manifestation of hysteria that recognizes no gender barriers.

The argument of Moi's Dora paper is ambitiously expanded in: 'Patriarchal Thought and the Drive for Knowledge' (1989). Like much of her earlier work, this paper begins with a careful re-examination of a widely accepted feminist position. Here she questions the argument of Evelyn Fox Keller's work on gender and science, which represents science, philosophy and other forms of structured thought based on the subject/object dichotomy as 'male', sexist and oppressive. Keller's alternative is knowledge that incorporates feeling, celebrates communion and welcomes women. This knowledge she calls 'female'. Moi begins her critique by objecting to Keller's use of the terms 'male' and 'female': Keller's simplistic polarization ignores the important fact that 'just as all women are not feminist, not all males are patriarchal' (*PT*, p. 190). Moi proceeds to argue that Keller's position is bound up with her commitment to Nancy Chodorow's object-relations theory, which Moi dismisses because it 'does not take the unconscious sufficiently into account, mistakenly rejects Freud's theory of drives as pure biologism, fails to theorize the difficult construction of subjectivity and sexual difference, neglects the contradictory and self-defeating nature of sexuality as theorized by Freud, and ends up idealizing the pre-Oedipal mother–child relationship' (*PT*, p. 191). Furthermore, Keller and Chodorow's sexist polarization of thought requires their suppressing Marx, Nietzsche, Freud, Heidegger, Wittgenstein and Derrida. 'Perhaps we are to think of them as "female" philosophers?' Moi quips (*PT*, p. 191). In place of Keller and Chodorow's timid advocacy of communion, which is little more than the revival of a European Romantic notion of the proper relationship of *man* and nature, Moi proposes a deconstruction of their essentialism that unfortunately has trapped them into an unexamined belief in self-identity and female identity. Moi finds the thought of Michèle Le Doeuff more epistemologically and politically productive.

Le Doeuff, in a paper entitled 'Women and Philosophy', reprinted in Moi's *French Feminist Thought*, finds a fundamental contradiction in traditional Western philosophy. The basis of philosophy is a pursuit or search for knowledge that simultaneously implies present lack and the promise of future completion. But women who would enter philosophy cannot openly proclaim their philosophical lack without being doubly bound and judged doubly wanting by the patriarchal imagination. According to this sexist caricature of the woman philosopher, she lacks a phallus and lacks a man. Because philosophy embodies desire for knowledge that requires its absence, a woman who declares her philosophical lack is thought simply to be pursuing philosophy as compensation for sexual frustration: 'she is taken to suffer from the *wrong* lack' (*PT*, p. 195). The other patriarchal possibility of caricature is to think, as Hegel did, of women's incapacity for philosophy as resulting from self-sufficient plenitude. Moi succinctly summarizes Hegel's position as one in which 'woman is an inferior thinker, . . . not because of her lack, but because of her lack of a lack' (*PT*, p. 195). Le Doeuff insists that philosophy must be aware of its unfinished nature in order to avoid the thoughtless oppositions of reason/unreason, masculinity/femininity and to think through its strategies of exclusion and premature closure. Moi, at this point, returns to Freud, Dora's case, problems of transference and counter-transference in psychoanalysis, and Lacan's participatory reading of Freud. She shows that Freud's understanding of epistemophilia, of the drive for knowledge, can provide an indispensable psychoanalytic base for anti-essentialist feminist philosophy of science:

> There is, then, in the psychoanalytic situation a model of knowledge which at once radically questions and displaces traditional notions of subject–object relationships and deconstructs the firm boundaries between knowledge and non-knowledge. (*PT*, p. 198)

Moi's own work displays this same avoidance of exclusivity and impatient finality. Although she has perfected the rhetoric of feminist critique, which is fundamental to all of her theoretical work, she carefully avoids allowing her method to become simply polemical or dismissive. Her desire is to advance feminist knowledge in the full recognition of its momentary lack. Not until the feminist struggle is won will that sense of lack vanish. But as feminism achieves its goal and becomes post-feminism, presumably, the momentum it has generated will be directed to overcoming other political and epistemological lacks. If one considers Moi's published work to date as forging links between feminism and psychoanalysis, deconstruction, and Marxism, it is that last connection (between feminism and Marxism) that would seem to await demonstration, despite the clarity of Moi's demonstration of its absence from feminist theory so far. Whether Moi's Marxism is the container or the contained, or less claustrophobically, whether feminism becomes, in her view, Marxism when it enters its post-patriarchal stage remains unclear. Moi has carefully shown how feminism virtually requires the theoretical insights of psychoanalysis and post-modernism, but she is yet to reclaim Marx for feminism in the same convincing detail with which she has reclaimed Freud. Presumably this is an awaiting task in her continuing project, a lack that for the moment contributes to its openness and dynamic expectation. Moi's current work on Simone de Beauvoir involves a new theoreticization of Beauvoir's position as an intellectual woman, based on the work of the French sociologist Pierre Bourdieu, a highly revisionist, but still recognizably *marxisant* theorist of cultural and intellectual life.

Michael Payne

REFERENCES

The following works by Toril Moi are cited in the Introduction:
'Representations of Patriarchy: Sexuality and Epistemology in Freud's *Dora*' (1981) (*RP*).
Sexual/Textual Politics: Feminist Literary Theory (1985) (*STP*).
(Ed.). *The Kristeva Reader* (1986) (*KR*).
(Ed.) *French Feminist Thought* (1987) (*FFT*).
'Feminism, Postmodernism and Style: Recent Feminist Criticism in the US' (1988) (*FPS*).
'Men Against Patriarchy', in Linda Kaufmann (ed.), *Gender and Theory: Dialogues on Feminist Criticism* (1989) (*MP*).
'Patriarchal Thought and the Drive for Knowledge', in Teresa Brennan (ed.), *Between Feminism and Psychoanalysis* (1989) (*PT*).

Politics and the Intellectual Woman: Clichés in the Reception of Simone de Beauvoir's Work

Quelle naïveté! Quel narcissisme!   (Audet, 1979)

Her passion-based politics turned Beauvoir into a ferocious enemy of France years ago.   (Chrestien, 1963)

For over sixty years, without a hitch and without a surprise, she played on her little instrument the same old tune, so suitable for a board of examiners.   (Bourdoiseau, 1986)

She never ceased being a docile pupil.   (Senart, 1963)

Her works, written with undeniable talent, are haughty, cold and dry. In this highly talented writer, the female intellectual has killed the generous resources of the heart. (Chaigne, 1954)

Simone de Beauvoir's naïveté has its source in a supreme and limiting egoism.   (Marks, 1973)

Simone de Beauvoir is not at all generous to her father. (Winegarten, 1988)

One should not go too easy on the simplistic manicheism of this female philosopher overcome by political passion as others are overcome by debauchery.   (Domaize, 1964)

Nothing is more tedious than lengthy accounts of previous research on some subject or other: cherished by conscientious thesis-writers, such papers tend to read like a series of grudgingly performed compulsory exercises standing between the writer and her own ideas. *The Interpretation of Dreams*, for instance, is far and away Freud's most popular book. But how many of us have actually read the awesome first chapter, enticingly entitled 'The Scientific Literature Dealing with the Problem of Dreams'? In this paper I make no attempt to survey the whole mass of existing literature on Simone de Beauvoir. So far, more than forty full-length studies have appeared, as well as hundreds of scholarly essays and massive newspaper and magazine coverage. Rather more limited in scope, my purpose here is simply to document and explore a particularly striking aspect in Beauvoir criticism: the unusual number of condescending, sarcastic, sardonic or dismissive accounts.[1] This hostile trend in the reception of Beauvoir's works has also been noticed by Elaine Marks, in the introduction to her thoroughly researched anthology, *Critical Essays on Simone de Beauvoir*:

> At least half of the critical essays I have included in this volume are, whether discreetly or obtrusively, sarcastic. They present Simone de Beauvoir as a slightly ridiculous figure, naive in her passions, sloppy in her scholarship, inaccurate in her documentation, generally out of her depth and inferior as a writer. Indeed the tone of superiority that many critics, of both sexes, adopt when writing about Simone de Beauvoir deserves special attention.   (p. 2)

Anne Whitmarsh, in her meticulous study of Beauvoir's political commitment, makes a somewhat similar point: 'Partisan judgments on the work of Simone de Beauvoir are the norm', she writes, 'tending to the extremes of either virulent attack or uncritical admiration' (1981, p. 2). My own view is that there is far more denigration and far less adulation than one might expect, and that a surprising number of critics must have invested considerable time and energy in a writer they plainly detest. Equally striking is the way in which well-intentioned or ostensibly 'neutral' writers, while willingly declaring their admiration for Beauvoir's work, almost imperceptibly and in spite of themselves move into a position of critical superiority. In a whole range of different contexts, then, Simone de Beauvoir's qualities as a person and as a writer are critically judged and found wanting.

Comparable French women writers are not treated in this way: nothing in the criticsm of say, Simone Weil, Marguerite Yourcenar, Marguerite Duras or Nathalie Sarraute matches the frequency and intensity of virulence displayed by so many of Simone de Beauvoir's critics. It is not easy for a feminist to deal with such an overwhelmingly hostile reception of a woman writer. There is an almost spontaneous desire to leap immediately to the wronged woman's defence, to assume that such critics *must* be patriarchal henchmen. But what if they could be shown to be right? Perhaps Simone de Beauvoir simply *is* an inferior writer? After all, no feminist could possibly object to an incisive discussion of difficult or dubious points in *any* writer's work. But this is not what is going on in Beauvoir criticism. As I will go on to show, the hostile critics' favourite strategy is to personalize the issues, to reduce the book to the woman: their aim is clearly to discredit Beauvoir as a speaker, not to enter into debate with her. To put it in the French linguist Emile Benveniste's terms: these critics are out to cast doubts on her right to posit herself as the subject of an *énonciation*, or in other words, her right to produce any kind of discourse. By discrediting her status as a speaker, they intend to preclude any further discussion of her actual statements, or *énoncés*.[2] In this situation, to defend Beauvoir is to do no more than to insist on her – and every other woman's – elementary democratic right to participate in the political, intellectual and literary debates of her time. It is only when this right has been firmly established that we can get on with the far more interesting task of analysing and criticizing Beauvoir's positions and views. In this paper, then, my defence of Beauvoir's right to intervene in the intellectual and political fields – *and to be taken seriously* – is absolute. To insist on this point is precisely to clear the ground for *real* discussion of her own highly complex and sometimes more than dubious positions.

To have to insist on women's right to speak today, more than forty years after the publication of *The Second Sex*, is disappointing, to say the least. Such was my naïve belief in progress, at least on this point, that I originally intended to organize this paper chronologically. The intention would have been to demonstrate how the reception of Beauvoir's works changed in different political contexts. Much to my chagrin I soon discovered that on the whole the very same sexist clichés surface unchanged from the 1950s to the 1980s: feminism has clearly not made that much of a difference, at least not in the French cultural climate. This paper, then, is an effort to document the deplorable persistence of these critical commonplaces and to analyse their implications. Beauvoir's uncertain status in the current French canon of literature, or what one would call her relative lack of *distinction*, will be discussed in my forthcoming book on Simone de Beauvoir.

Not even Beauvoir criticism, however, is wholly dominated by hostility. The first study ever published, Geneviève Gennari's warm and admiring *Simone de Beauvoir*, appeared in 1958, the year in which Beauvoir published the first volume of her autobiography. The publication of *Memoirs of a Dutiful Daughter* spurred several committed Catholics to write about her as the great lost daughter of the Catholic Church. Out to oppose Beauvoir's philosophical views, these sexist (and, it must be said, male) authors (Henry, Hourdin, and Gagnebin) nevertheless emphasize their respect and admiration for Beauvoir's *oeuvre* and in no way come across as particularly hostile. There are also two sympathetic existentialist and/or socialist studies from the 1960s (Jeanson and Julienne-Caffié) and, as might be expected, a fair number of reasonably open-minded studies of a more or less scholarly kind. Beauvoir has also inspired a series of popular (and sometimes sensationalist) works intended for a non-academic market, ranging from the truly appalling *Hearts and Minds* by Axel Madsen to the somewhat sugary and glamorizing, but still readable biography by Claude Francis and Fernande Gonthier, and the serviceable presentation of her life and work by Lisa Appignanesi.

In the 1980s, Beauvoir studies have shifted decisively away from France as well as from so-called mainstream preoccupations with political and philosophical themes. Before 1980, Beauvoir critics were predominantly French: only five out of an estimated twenty-one full-length studies were published in English. The first English-language study, Elaine Marks's *Simone de Beauvoir: Encounters with Death*, did not appear until 1973. From 1980 to 1988, however, of thirteen books devoted to Beauvoir, ten appeared in English. Of the remaining three, two were written by French academics working in the United States (Zéphir and Francis and Gonthier), and the third is not a study, but a personal memoir written by a friend of Beauvoir's, Françoise d'Eaubonne. Never strong (a few short theses, a couple of books intended for *lycée* students), intellectual interest in Simone de Beauvoir in France now seems almost non-existent. The one remarkable exception to this rule is the French feminist philosopher Michèle Le Doeuff and her incisive essays on Beauvoir's difficult relationship to philosophy as well as her brilliant study *L'étude et le rouet* where Beauvoir is discussed in the context of women's relationship to philosophy in general.

There are some obvious reasons for this well-nigh total desertion of Beauvoir by the French: in the 1970s and 1980s French intellectual fashions (structuralism, post-structuralism, Lacanian psychoanalysis, post-modernism) have left no space at all for an unreconstructed existentialist humanist of Beauvoir's type. Post-structuralist feminist theory in France, as represented by Hélène Cixous, Luce Irigaray and Julia Kristeva for instance, has had very little to say about the author of *The Second Sex*. Indeed, the group round *politique et psychanalyse* always considered her a phallic woman, complicit with the dominant forms of masculine power. Interviewed by the left-wing newspaper *Libération* the day after Beauvoir's death in April 1986, Antoinette Fouque, the leading light of *Psych et Po*, expresses her hostility towards the author of *The Second Sex*: 'Only one month ago', Fouque says, 'she was giving interviews in order to assert her universalist, egalitarian, assimilatory and normalizing feminist positions, roundly attacking anybody who did not fall into line' (p. 5). The gist of Fouque's argument is that now that Beauvoir is dead, feminism is finally free to move into the twenty-first century.

In Beauvoir studies, then, the 1980s are the decade of Anglo-American feminism. But Beauvoir proves controversial for British and American feminists as well. Some feminists take up a hostile or disappointed position (Leighton, Evans), some verge on the adulatory (Ascher), whereas others produce highly judicious feminist accounts of her work (Okeley, Fallaize). When men write on Beauvoir in the 1980s, it tends to be because they too are interested in feminism (Zéphir, Hatcher).[3] Although it is difficult to overestimate the importance of Beauvoir's feminist work, it may look as if the critics of the 1980s have neglected other aspects of her *oeuvre*. Whatever the importance of *The Second Sex*, it ought not to be forgotten that until she was well over sixty, Beauvoir did not think of herself as a feminist at all.[4]

While helping to construct a relatively nuanced picture, close scrutiny of Beauvoir criticism does nothing to weaken the reader's impression that the reception of her work is more hostile than might reasonably be expected. What is it about Beauvoir that produces this effect? Why do so many readers find themselves stirred to the point of irritation or even rage? How does one account for such *reading-effects* as these, regularly produced by Beauvoir's texts? These questions are too wide-ranging to be fully explored here: only detailed study of individual texts can start to furnish some kind of answer. But if some of the answers must be sought in her texts, it also remains true that the critics' preconceptions or prejudices and their own political, theoretical and ideological positions structure their readings for them. Here I want simply to focus on certain recurring themes in hostile responses to Beauvoir, and as far as possible try to detect the critics' own *parti pris*, or in other words, the position that structures their particular response to Beauvoir.

Reducing the Book to the Woman

It is impossible to read much hostile Beauvoir criticism without noticing the recurrence of certain *topoi*, or commonplaces. 'Books by women are treated as though they themselves were women, and criticism embarks, at its happiest, upon an intellectual measuring of busts and hips', Mary Ellmann notes (*Thinking About Women*, p. 29). In the case of Simone de Beauvoir, her political and philosophical positions are treated in this way as well. It is as if the very fact of her femaleness blocks any further discussion of the issues at stake, be they literary, theoretical or political. Instead the critic obsessively returns to the question of femininity, or more specifically to what one might call the *personality topos*, passionately discussing Beauvoir's looks, character, private life or morality. The implication is that whatever a woman says, or writes, or thinks, is less important and less interesting than what she *is*.

It is in this context that the figure of the *midinette*, or shop-girl, makes her appearance. In France, the *midinette* has inescapable connotations to shallow superficiality and sentimentality. The *Petit Robert* defines the term as 'simple and frivolous city-girl'.[5] The *midinette topos* reaches its most dignified expression in Claude Lévi-Strauss's *Tristes tropiques*, where in splendidly patriarchal manner he accuses existentialism in general of being nothing more than a kind of 'shop-girl metaphysics' (*métaphysique pour midinette*), since its so-called thought is simply the 'promotion of personal preoccupations to the dignity of philosophical problems' (p. 61). As for Beauvoir, 'When she travels, she's a shop-girl sending postcards to her family: "wonderful views!"', one journalist writes about *Adieux: A Farewell to Sartre*. The same reporter, in what is surely the most distasteful reference to Beauvoir to be found anywhere,[6] does not shrink from comparing Beauvoir to Milou, the dog belonging to the well-known cartoon-figure Tintin: 'Today, evidence in hand, one may be allowed to think that Simone de Beauvoire was Milou. A Milou who a year after Tintin's disappearance would lift his leg on his golf-trousers'.[7] Another, reviewing *Les Belles Images* in *L'Express*, insists on reading the text in the light of the 'two opposing poles of Simone de Beauvoir's personality: the austere philosopher and the sentimental shop-girl'.[8] Bernard Pivot sounds the same note when he labels Simone de Beauvoir 'une vraie femme de lettres (pour le courrier du coeur)', or 'a true woman of letters (for the agony column)'.[9] The right-wing extremist Robert Poulet goes even further and declares that *all* literary ladies ('ces dames') including Beauvoir are *midinettes en diable* (p. 174).

Many critics first reduce every text by Beauvoir to her own *persona*, and then go on to declare that such autobiographical effusions cannot be considered *art* at all. Such involvement with one's own life, they argue, is no more than a kind of pedestrian labour of documentation, more akin to history than to literature. Brian T. Fitch claims that *She Came to Stay* is so autobiographical that it cannot be considered a 'work of art existing in itself'; its interest is more a matter for literary history than for literary criticism, he adds (p. 13). Not surprisingly, he concludes that Simone de Beauvoir lacks imagination (p. 149). Robert Poulet sees *The Mandarins* as a typical 'female novel', that is to say as desperately confessional and extremely uninteresting (see pp. 173–4). 'In fact' he continues:

> almost all these amazons of science, of thought or of politics pay for their spiritual independence with a kind of secret infantilism. . . . The female temper is not made for freedom: in order to make the most of its exquisiteness, it needs limits and constraints. Every time one hoists a daughter of Eve on to a summit, she behaves badly and says silly things. . . . To put it frankly, [Simone de Beauvoir] is not at all a strong woman, but a timid, hesitant and nostalgic being who forces herself to march with a determined step under the helmet of her artificially hardened cerebrality. (pp. 174–5)

One critic demonstrates an unusually intense urge to reduce everything Beauvoir wrote to a distasteful expression of her personality. In this sense Jean-Raymond Audet comes across as a particularly extreme example of a widespread trend in Beauvoir criticism. His *Simone de Beauvoir face à la mort* would seem to be motivated entirely by some kind of sexist *ressentiment* against her, rather than by more specific political grudges. Insisting that *all* of Beauvoir's fictional characters (but particularly the female ones) 'are' Beauvoir herself, Audet – and the plethora of other critics who have recourse to the same strategy – proceeds to attribute every possible vice to the hapless author, including that of perversely attributing her own psychology to her characters. Needless to say, the circularity of this 'argument' is no deterrent. Heavily reliant on Elaine

Marks's much more thoughtful work on the topic, Audet's study of Beauvoir and death is quite fanatic in its efforts to demonstrate that Beauvoir herself is narcissistic, egoistic and naïve: 'What naïvety! What narcissism! And what an obsessional desire [*manie*] to endow her characters with all the vicissitudes of her own psychological, sociological and political development!' (p. 91).

According to Audet, Beauvoir *is* not only Françoise (of *She Came to Stay*) (p. 49), but the neurotic actress Régine of *All Men are Mortal* – 'an eminently faithful portrait of our author', he comments (p. 102) – in fact, she *is* every single character she ever invented, including the protagonists of the 1960s fiction, such as Monique in 'The Woman Destroyed', a housewife who has never had an independent career and who has a nervous breakdown when her husband of twenty years leaves her; and Murielle in 'The Monologue', a woman who drove her teenage daughter to suicide, and now is verging on the psychotic in her self-indulgent torrent of imprecations and denunciation of her family, ex-friends and ex-lovers. The anorexic advertising executive, Laurence, in *Les Belles Images* is another faithful representation of Beauvoir's personality, Audet claims. Had Beauvoir chosen to write about the harsh lives of nomadic Bedouin women, one feels sure that Audet would have claimed them as egocentric portraits of the author as well. In *All Said and Done*, Beauvoir comments on the way in which many readers strenuously seek to equate her with these characters:

Yet many readers claim that they see me in all my female characters. Laurence in *Les Belles Images*, disgusted with life to the point of anorexia is supposed to be me. The angry university-woman in 'The Age of Discretion' is also supposed to be me. . . . And of course 'The Woman Destroyed' could not be anyone but myself. . . . One woman wrote to ask whether the chairwoman of her literary club was right in saying that Sartre had broken with me.

Replying to questioners, my friend Stépha pointed out that I was no longer forty, that I had no daughters, and that my life was unlike Monique's in every way. They allowed themselves to be convinced. 'But', said one of them crossly, 'Why does she fix it so that all her novels seem to be autobiographical?' 'She's only trying to make them ring true', replied Stépha.   (p. 144/180–1)

It is amusing to see how a critic of Audet's calibre tries to get round this statement, not to mention the texts themselves. Having quoted the passage reproduced here, his only comment is a smug and self-satisfied: 'Quelle naïve candeur!' (p. 122). In fact, he says, he totally agrees with the 'chairwoman of the literary club', because what else than a break with Sartre could have produced the filthy language of 'The Monologue'? As for *Les Belles Images*, he is even more inventive: 'This time we will not try to show that Laurence is Simone de Beauvoir', he triumphantly exclaims: 'For who else can she be?' (p. 125).

A traditional Romantic critic might have tried to turn Beauvoir's apparently endless capacity for projecting herself into a wide range of fictional characters into grounds for praise, comparing her to Shakespeare ('myriad-minded Beauvoir!'). This *never* happens in Beauvoir criticism. Whenever the *topos* of the author's projection of herself into her fiction crops up, it is always in order to demonstrate her regrettable *limitations*. In particular it is invoked to 'prove' that Beauvoir as a person and as a writer is narcissistic, egocentric and arrogant: she is only interested in herself. Such extraordinary claims assume, firstly, that Beauvoir in fact always writes about herself; secondly, that she always approves of all her characters as perfect incarnations of her own virtues (it should hardly be necessary to say that both assumptions are demonstrably false); and thirdly – by far the most important point – that to show any sign of self-satisfaction is a bad thing in a woman.

The very fact of writing a multi-volume autobiography, for example, is presented as evidence of her relentless narcissism. It may be necessary to point out that this is not generally the reaction to male autobiography. While not hesitating to call Elias Canetti egoistic, a recent review of his autobiography (so far it runs to three volumes), first signals Canetti's self-involvement: 'Canetti is interested in his fellows only for the discoveries they might lead him to; what compassion there is in his work is mostly reserved for himself. . . . His descriptions of others are rarely sweetened by generosity' (Campbell p. 926), only to turn such self-involvement into a virtue:

> But although Canetti is one of the great egoists of literature, to dwell on his vanity would blind us to his true purpose, which is to convey the reality of the inner life in all its aspects. Flitting among many genres, he remakes each in his own image; he is constantly surprised by his perception, and the record is of a man charting new ways of experiencing himself.   (p. 926)

Spanning many genres and comprising both travel writing and autobiography, Beauvoir's *oeuvre* is in some ways similar to Canetti's. In her case, however, not only is the fact that she often writes in autobiographical genres used as evidence of her debilitating egocentricity; her discussions of traditional 'non-personal' topics, such as politics and philosophy, tend to be disparaged as mere displacements of the personal.[10] A favourite variation on this theme is the tendency to perceive Beauvoir's writings as the simple effect of her personal relationship to Sartre. Her emotional ties to him explain her texts, it is claimed; there is thus no need to assume that she possesses much creativity or insight of her own. When she received an important Austrian literary prize in 1979, *Figaro Magazine* came up with the following headline: 'A perfect bourgeoise: Simone de Beauvoir. Simone de Beauvoir, the first woman to receive the Austrian Prize for European Literature, owes everything to a man.'[11] On her death, *Le Monde* ran an article entitled 'Her works: popularization rather than creation.'[12]

Using the Personal to Discredit the Political

As might be expected, a politically outspoken woman such as Beauvoir attracts much hostility from her political opponents on the left as well as on the right. Paradoxically, however, politically motivated critiques of Beauvoir contain surprisingly little discussion of politics and much apparently pointless dwelling on her personality and private life. In fact such dwelling on her personality is best described as the politicized use of the sexist personality *topos*. The intended effect is to *depoliticize* her by presenting her political choices not as the outcome of careful reflection on the issues at stake, but as the inexplicable *élans* of an overemotional or even hysterical woman. Having reduced his opponent to a woman with personal problems, the hostile critic then avoids having to reveal – and defend – his or her own politics.

The dividing line between sexist and other forms of political uses of this rhetorical strategy can never be clear: in many cases – whether intentionally or not – an ambiguous double effect is produced. Particularly efficient in this respect is the use of the patriarchal cliché of the 'unfeminine woman'. Beauvoir is regularly represented as cold, selfish, egocentric and uncaring, and above all as *non-maternal*. 'She is totally devoid of the triple instinct with which woman is endowed', a female Catholic comments in 1984; 'the maternal instinct, the nurturing instinct, and the nest-building instinct'.[13] Mobilized in political contexts, this *topos* is used to imply that her political commitment is devoid of normal concern for the well-being of the human race. However much Beauvoir herself emphasizes her opposition to exploitation, oppression and suffering, she is suspected of not 'really' caring for the suffering of every victim of every conflict in the world.

Hardly ever used against male politicians, this specific rhetorical strategy is deeply dishonest. It tends to be assumed that men take difficult political decisions with reluctance, weighed down by the burden of their heavy responsibilities. Churchill, Roosevelt or de Gaulle were never suspected of lacking ordinary human feelings every time they imposed costly sacrifices on their men. Even Sartre rarely gets attacked for his lack of humanity.[14] If Simone de Beauvoir tends to be accused of callousness by her political opponents, it would seem primarily to be because she is a woman who refuses to remain confined to the private sphere. Beauvoir, then, is regularly put in a classic double bind: if she writes about politics, she is told that she is cold, unfeeling and unfeminine, but also that her political ideas are simple displacements of her own emotional problems. If she actually writes about her own emotions, however, she is immediately accused of being selfish or unartistic. Like Virginia Woolf, Beauvoir pays dearly indeed for the sin of not being the incarnation of the ultimate non-writing woman, the Angel in the House.

A recent example of right-wing efforts to mobilize the personal in order to discredit the political can be found in Renée Winegarten's study with the somewhat understated title *Simone de Beauvoir: A Critical View*. Steeped in Reaganism, Winegarten's essay usefully demonstrates that Beauvoir has lost none of her power to threaten the *bienpensants* of this world. Rarely missing a chance to present Beauvoir as domineering and narrow-minded, Winegarten strives to reproduce that perennial patriarchal favourite, the *topos* of the *mégère* – the shrew or the harridan. The whole book, in fact, reads as a sustained attempt to produce the impression that Sartre spent most of his time trying to dodge Simone's never-ending harassment. The clinching evidence of Beauvoir's efforts to gain total power over her companion appears in the last paragraph of the book, which starts by presenting Beauvoir's funeral (5000 participants) as altogether less impressive than Sartre's (50,000). One might just as well insist that her funeral was a massive event compared to that of Michel Foucault.[15] Having made her telling comparison, Winegarten goes on to paraphrase the well-known story of how Beauvoir tried to lie down under the sheet covering Sartre's dead body:

> A nurse dissuaded her, because gangrene had already set in. Instead, she lay down on top of the sheet. In this act of high melodrama, she made one of the last of her attempts to claim him. Even in death he contrived to evade her total control and her desire to impose upon posterity the image of an ideal union, just as he had in life. (p. 121)

Winegarten's primary concern, however, is to present Beauvoir's political positions as utterly irrational, and therefore as further evidence of her extraordinary naïvety, self-deception and lack of ordinary human qualities such as care and compassion for others. Her principal strategy is not openly to oppose her views, to meet Beauvoir head-on in the political arena, but to present her political decisions as the result of male influence and deep self-deception, and in any case as defying logic, common sense and so-called 'human values'. In Winegarten's text, the *topos* of the *hysteric* – the irrational, overemotional female – is skilfully blended with that of the harridan or shrew. Beauvoir's socialism, for instance, is reduced to a symptom of personal conflicts: 'If she remained unceasing in her opposition to the bourgeoisie', Winegarten writes, 'it was doubtless because she heard in it her father's voice' (p. 15). If it isn't Sartre or her father who is responsible for her political commitment, it is some other man, usually a lover. Her rejection of US politics in the McCarthy era is blamed on Nelson Algren, the Chicago novelist:

> He was among those oversimplifiers who were convinced
> of the decay of capitalism, and whose sympathies lay with
> the cause of revolution. . . . What he did was to show her
> the worst and darkest side of American life, confirm her
> prejudices, and inculcate an extreme view of the country
> as one of exploiters and exploited, a view from which she
> would never depart, and which would harden with the
> years.   (pp. 68–9)

Summarizing the whole experience as Beauvoir's 'slumming
with Algren' (p. 69), Winegarten clearly thinks that only
a woman blinded by erotic passion could believe that
American society were made up of exploiters and exploited.
As they say in the Soviet Union: 'Capitalism is the
exploitation of man by man; socialism is just the opposite.'

As for Beauvoir's position on the Israeli–Arab conflict,
according to Winegarten, her blind support for Algerian
violence during the Algerian war of independence (1954–62)
might have made her take up a naïve pro-Palestinian
position, but luckily she 'had been influenced by her liaison
with Claude Lanzmann, a keen Zionist' (p. 77), and so
was saved from further political aberrations on this front.
The fact that Beauvoir's unwavering support for Israel's
right of existence dates right back to 1948, whereas she
did not meet Lanzmann until 1952, is conveniently left
unmentioned.

To Winegarten, Beauvoir's strong anti-imperialist stance
comes across as utterly incomprehensible. How could she
exult at her own country's defeat in Indo-China and
Algeria? Clearly utterly baffled by the whole question, the
critic reveals herself to be wholly in the grips of Reaganite
nationalism. To mask her disarray, however, she tries to
make Beauvoir look like an overemotional hypocrite:

> Throughout the autobiography, there runs an account of
> her reactions to political affairs in which others were
> actively engaged: her anxiety, her indignation, her anger,

her tears, her pain and horror at the suffering of the victims, her disaffection, even her 'satisfaction' at the humiliating French defeat at Dien Bien Phu which ended the war in Indochina. This emotional response, accompanied by a disinclination to participate in the political process of French democracy, gives constant proof of her sense of her right feelings while freeing her from responsibility in any decisions that are taken. . . . Such intellectual hatred of her culture and civilisation while at the same time serving it through her literary efforts is difficult to appreciate. It is a type of alienation that has grown more common.   (pp. 119–20)

The explanation which eludes Winegarten is, first, the fact that during the Algerian war Beauvoir and Sartre considered de Gaulle's regime as a military dictatorship, on a par with that of Pétain. For them, to participate in such government, as André Malraux did, was tantamount to betraying, not upholding, democracy. Nor did they believe, as Winegarten apparently does, that France, the colonial power, represented *democracy* to the vast majority of Vietnamese or Algerians.

As for Beauvoir's anti-bourgeois position, Winegarten is convinced that to hold such a view is tantamount to aligning oneself with Hitler's final solution, or perhaps more accurately, with Stalin's onslaught on the kulaks. At least she earnestly claims that Beauvoir and Sartre 'sought the actual liquidation of an entire class' (p. 12), presumably including themselves. Undeterred, she has more to say on this subject:

The worst aspect of this Marxian standpoint is that people are no longer judged as individuals with a share of virtues and shortcomings, but solely as the representatives of an evil, exploitative class or mass. In effect, it resembles the bias of judging people to be harmful because of their race or religion, a view which Simone de Beauvoir otherwise abhorred. On the subject of the bourgeois class, however, she could see no redeeming feature whatsoever, and this prejudice colours her entire work.   (p. 8)

Or in other words: socialists are incapable of understanding – let alone sympathizing with – individual human emotions; and to accept a Marxist analysis of exploitation is tantamount to becoming a racist as well.

Winegarten is particularly fond of the stereotype of the cold, unfeeling, inhuman, political woman. To her, the passage in *A Very Easy Death* where Beauvoir compares her mother's death in a private hospital in Paris with the far harsher circumstances surrounding the death of the poor and underprivileged in French society, is chilling evidence that Beauvoir sacrificed every normal human feeling on the altar of her embittered and misunderstood socialism. What Beauvoir writes is this:

> For indeed, comparatively speaking her death was an easy one. 'Don't leave me in the power of the brutes.' I thought of all those who have no one to make that appeal to: what agony it must be to feel oneself a defenceless thing, utterly at the mercy of indifferent doctors and overworked nurses. . . . Even today – why? – there are horrible agonizing deaths. And then in the public wards, when the last hour is coming near, they put a screen round the dying man's bed: he has seen this screen round other beds that were empty the next day: he knows. I pictured Maman, blinded for hours by the black sun that no one can look at directly: the horror of her staring eyes with their dilated pupils. She had a very easy death; an upper-class death.   (p. 83/135–6)

Above all an impassioned protest against death *tout court*, regardless of class distinctions, *A Very Easy Death* is also a compassionate plea for better hospitals and nursing facilities for the poor. Winegarten, however, can see nothing but a daughter's unfeeling class vendetta against her dying mother:

She could not resist comparing the manner of her mother's death, however, with that of the aged poor who die alone and neglected, remarking that her mother had been cherished and well-cared-for as a 'privileged' person. Though strictly true, the very observation still strikes chill. (pp. 15–16)

Readings such as Winegarten's do not come across as entirely disinterested exercises. Winegarten herself, however, insists that she is out to correct Beauvoir's false views, to *demystify* the ideological aberrations of her subject in the name of truth:

One will find in the present undertaking neither the surrogate mother-figure, cherished by those individuals in quest of feminine identity, nor the idol of the utopian revolutionary Left. . . . This study offers rather an attempt to probe the mystifications of an all-too-common modern form of rationalism which leads its adherents to see only what they wish to see, where change and revolution are at stake – whether in personal or public relations. (p. 6)

The rhetorical move here is obvious: the cumbersome periphrasis 'an all-too-common modern form of rationalism' is deployed as a trope destined to mask Winegarten's real target: any form of socialism or Marxism. Against the impaired eyesight of modern Marxists, she sets her own superior insights into the *true* nature of things. It goes without saying that where Beauvoir is blinkered and ideological. Winegarten is impartial and *right*. In this she remains faithful to the everyday definition of ideology, as summarized by Terry Eagleton:

To accuse someone of speaking ideologically, in common or garden speech, is surely to claim that they are judging a particular object or situation through a rigid framework of preconceived ideas which distorts their understanding.

I view things as they really are; you squint at them through
a tunnel vision imposed by some extraneous body of
doctrine. There is usually a suggestion here that this tunnel
vision leads you to an over-simplifying view of the world
– that to judge or speak 'ideologically' is to do so
schematically, stereotypically, and maybe with the faintest
touch of fanatical extremism. The opposite of 'ideological'
here would thus be less 'absolute truth' than 'pragmatic'
or 'empirical'.[16]

It ought no longer to be necessary to insist on the false
epistemology at work in positions such as Winegarten's, to
argue that she cannot possibly claim to have truth where
Beauvoir only has ideology. Whatever else Winegarten's
thinly veiled defence of imperialism, capitalism and
exploitative individualism, may be, it surely is not impartial.
The truly ideological move in Winegarten's discourse is
above all the way in which she tries to pass her own
political prejudices off as universal truths, or more
insidiously: as *common sense*.

Judicious Balance: Liberalism and Human Sympathy

Liberal critics tend not to define themselves as political.
For them, too, ideology is always something somebody
else suffers from, never a constraint on their own discourse.
Explicitly setting out to produce independent-minded
scholarly studies free from political bias and other forms
of prejudice, liberals do not necessarily come across as
noticeably more friendly towards Simone de Beauvoir than
the right-wingers. This is partly because they too tend to
draw heavily on the personality *topos*, and partly because
these mild-mannered critics tend to find Beauvoir's
explicitly political and conflictual world-view particularly
infuriating. Unfortunately, Beauvoir's passionate refusal of
traditional essentialism, as well as her tendency to hold

even moderate beliefs extremely only serves to alienate these critics further. Not surprisingly, then, their favourite invectives against her are 'dogmatic' or 'extremist'.

On the whole, liberal critics tend to express their disapproval of Beauvoir not as a general critique of her basic positions, but in a relatively fragmented point-by-point way. In many cases there is nothing wrong with this: if a critic has gone to the trouble of presenting a painstakingly detailed reading of a text, it is only to be expected that she will comment on contradictions, inconsistencies and flaws wherever she finds them. Not infrequently, however, there is a puzzling contradiction between the critic's explicit stance of well-intentioned judiciousness and the overwhelming amount of potentially damning critique she actually produces. The rhetorical effect of such a double stance is to give the impression that the *true* picture of Beauvoir has finally emerged: if even an impartial critic's conclusions are damning it must be because they are *right*. In this way, like Winegarten, these critics too come to reproduce what Terry Eagleton calls the 'common or garden' definition of ideology.

Terry Keefe, for instance, laments the fact that too much emphasis on Beauvoir's feminism and her relationship with Sartre 'has often resulted in a distorted picture of Beauvoir as a writer'. Explicitly setting out to provide a balanced study to rectify the distortions (p. 5), he is honest enough to own up to a certain unease about the nature of his own conclusions: 'Anyone approaching Beauvoir's writings with a reasonably open mind has a very great deal to gain', he writes, 'and I hope that this emerges from the following pages, even where criticism of her ideas and literary achievements is severe' (p. 5). In fact his book is packed with grudging comments on Beauvoir's texts. Here are some random examples: *Old Age* is full of 'over-generalisations and exaggerations' that 'anyone can recognize' (p. 137); '*Privilèges* as a whole is a very unsatisfactory work' (p. 123); 'It is not difficult to spot misjudgements and distorted emphases in *America Day by Day*, too much space is devoted to descriptions of night-clubs' (p. 55). As for the memoirs: 'Taken together, the four volumes do not have the harmony, the shape, or even the quality of writing that would make them a major artistic achievement' (p. 50), Keefe claims. As might be expected by now, *The Second Sex* is not safe either: in fact, it 'leaves a good deal to be desired, for the book cannot be said to be very carefully composed, or even, on the whole, particularly well-written' (p. 111).

Such nit-picking at least has the unexpected effect of making the grand ideological condemnations of the right-wingers seem positively entertaining in comparison. Keefe's final conclusion is that Beauvoir's essays are 'emphatic' and 'sweeping' (p. 228); that many of her novels '*do* have such obvious aesthetic defects that one may be disinclined even to consider whether they are accomplished works of art' (p. 229); and that her autobiographical texts 'mostly leave us *such* strong impressions of contingency and facticity that we are easily drawn into reading them for the information of various kinds that they convey than for anything else' (p. 229). Grudgingly granting that there are exceptions to these rules, Beauvoir is then rated as a 'writer of some stature', albeit one whose work is marred by 'a distinctive kind of fragility or vulnerability' (p. 229).

In his *Histoire vivante de la littérature d'aujourd'hui, 1938–58*, a work that aims to present a reasonably objective panorama of contemporary French literature, Pierre de Boisdeffre allots far more space to Beauvoir than to any other French woman writer – indeed, far more than to the great majority of male writers discussed. Again there is a curious tension between the claim that Beauvoir is among the most important writers of her time and the rather uncharitable conclusions reached by the critic. On the one hand *She Came to Stay* is 'one of the best *récits* to have appeared in France in the wake of *Nausea*' (p. 111); on the other, Boisdeffre's praise is laced with disapproval:

'Who could deny the almost masculine strength and power of this novelist, the virility of an intelligence that obstinately refuses to let go, to yield to grace or even to the narcissism of her own nature?' (p. 269). If Beauvoir is not truly important as a writer after all, it would seem to be mostly because of her regrettable lack of femininity: 'It is not in intelligence or talent that Simone de Beauvoir is lacking, but perhaps in the humility required to receive the spontaneous gifts of life. . . . Marked by a wholly masculine ambition, her work gives rise to curiosity without exerting true influence' (p. 117).[17]

Elaine Marks's *Simone de Beauvoir: Encounters with Death*, an excellent example of liberal criticism, was published in 1973, well before feminism hit Beauvoir studies. It ought to be pointed out that Marks's later feminist work on Beauvoir is noticeable for its incisive and fair-minded approach (see, for, instance *Critical Essays* and 'Transgressing the (In)cont(in)ent Boundaries'). Serious and well researched, Marks's study also deploys an original and powerful methodological move – to juxtapose passages from different texts, often from different genres, dealing with the same experience – which is strikingly successful in shedding new light on neglected connections between various aspects of Beauvoir's work. It cannot be denied, however, that her study in effect amounts to a scathing condemnation of Beauvoir herself, as well as her texts. As her argument proceeds, consciously or unconsciously, Mark's tone becomes increasingly hostile: in the second half of her book references to Beauvoir's 'pathological egotism' (p. 81), 'hysterical mode of reaction' (p. 95) and 'grotesque evasions' (p. 99) abound.

Marks's main argument is that Beauvoir's work constitutes one long meditation on death. Obsessed with death, returning time and time again to the topic, Beauvoir nevertheless fails fully to confront it; her work in fact becomes one long series of 'evasions' of death. Marks's summary of her findings is bleak:

The arguments and the flight are doomed. The body of her writings is a 'meditation on death'; all her themes and elaborations are pretexts for the endless wrestling with her own mortality, of which she is acutely aware but which she has no means, emotional or intellectual, of confronting without hysteria or ideology. (p. 126)

In other words: Beauvoir is egocentric, emotionally and intellectually inadequate, and prone to hysterical and ideological distortions of reality as well. It can be shown, I think, that Marks's distaste for Simone de Beauvoir is not simply idiosyncratic or coincidental, but a logical consequence of her unswerving loyalty to an unusually purified and abstract form of humanism. Marks sees Beauvoir's work as split by the tension between the sense of the absurd, defined as 'the feeling of emptiness at the heart of all things', on the one hand; and the 'desperate need to fill the emptiness, more commonly referred to as commitment', on the other (p. 3). This opposition, Marks argues, produces two different literary styles: the first, of which she wholeheartedly approves, focuses on the absurd, and seeks to describe 'things in the world as they are' (p. 3). The other is the rhetoric of commitment, which unfortunately also has its own deplorable aesthetics:

The rhythm of commitment is busy and regulated. Its tone, concerned, humorless, optimistic is never ironic; its language, rhetorical and oracular, is solemn, full of confidence and conviction. The major theme is unity and the point of view is always moral, social, and political.

Gratuity, the monarch in the universe of the absurd, is replaced by usefulness, play by total activity, analysis by synthesis, phenomenology by ideology. In the leap from the absurd to commitment, from death to history, a concrete problem is given abstract answers. (pp. 3–4)

While the style of the absurd produces 'moments of

heightened intensity, rigorous descriptions of sensations and sentiments; pitiless and poignant analyses of weaknesses' (p. 4), commitment, according to Marks, simply produces bad prose: 'an often mediocre, vulgar journalese in which endless explanations of the obvious and simpering moralistic clichés annoy and embarrass the reader' (p. 4). Marks's conclusion is not in the least intended as irony: 'Death and the absurd', she declares, 'are always more elegant and refined than history and commitment' (p. 4). True aesthetic refinement, in other words, is incompatible with political engagement, in Beauvoir's *oeuvre* as everywhere else. Art must have nothing to do with history: 'ideology' as opposed to the direct contemplation of 'things as they are' inevitably produces bad writing. Given this starting point, Mark's conclusions are predictable: since Beauvoir persists in juxtaposing existential anguish and social and political activity, she is 'annoyingly' and 'embarrassingly' sacrificing universal truths on the altar of history.

Marks's strange insistence on the absolute *opposition* of death and history leads her to argue that contemplation of the metaphysical absurdity of death is *concrete*, whereas history, normally considered the arena where men and women live and die, is *abstract*. Her profound belief in the supreme reality of unchanging human essences could not emerge more clearly. It is this belief, radically opposed to Beauvoir's own philosophical concerns, that makes her reject any concern with politics, society or history, or indeed with *human community*, as ideological obscurantism.

Marks's peculiar definition of concreteness allows her to label every death described by Beauvoir as 'abstract'. In the end the reader must wonder whether any death, short of one's own, could possibly qualify as 'concrete' enough. In *Memoirs of a Dutiful Daughter*, for example, Beauvoir describes her despair when as a little girl she learnt of the death of their servant Louise's baby, a scene that for her is inextricably tied up with the poverty of Louise's surroundings (see p. 131/182–3). To Marks, such a reaction is an evasion of the fact of death; it is, she argues, 'less an encounter with death than an encounter with "society", a human and therefore a remediable injustice' (p. 41). In the *Blood of Others* Beauvoir makes another mistake, that of wanting to *particularize* death:

> By presenting each death as a particular phenomenon due to specific causes: poverty, political action, the Resistance movement; by refusing to generalize – all men die – or to identify – the narrator never thinks of himself as mortal – Simone de Beauvoir has led her characters, her readers, and herself astray. (p. 40)

Such strategies deprive us of an 'uncluttered view of death' (p. 41), Marks complains. Nothing short of unswerving contemplation of absolute death will do. As long as Beauvoir refuses to comply with this demand, she is accused of being uncaring and unfeeling. Her disarray at the death of Louise's baby, Marks argues, is socially induced 'guilt', not pure anguish, and thus does not count as true sympathy. For Marks, to reach out to other people in a solidarity transcending strictly individualist concerns is to betray the dead.

On Marks's logic, it does not matter *who* dies, what matters is abstract and universal death. Beauvoir's 'egoism' in fact consists in refusing to acknowledge this superior insight as truth. Nowhere, Marks argues, is her lack of common humanity more evident than in her distasteful condemnation of fascists and collaborators. It is true that Beauvoir was in favour of the death penalty, and in a highly complex essay first published in 1946, 'Oeil pour oeil' ('Eye for Eye'), she argues in favour of the execution of Robert Brasillach, the anti-Semitic editor of the fascist review *Je suis partout*. During the Occupation, Brasillach used to publish the names and addresses of Jews in hiding from the police. In 'Oeil pour Oeil', Beauvoir weighs the arguments for and against the death penalty for collaborators. One problem, she says, is that collaborators are brought to justice in a political situation radically different from that in which they committed their crimes. It is therefore difficult to see them as the hated power-figures they were; instead they tend to appear as lonely victims of a new order: 'We desired the death of the editor of *Je suis partout*', she writes, 'not the death of this man so eager to die well' ('Oeil', p. 149). Marks's commentary takes the liberal confidence in absolute and essential humanity to new heights:

> But the editor-in-chief of *Je suis partout* was and could only be a man, as Mussolini, Darnand, Hitler, Balue, and the assassins of Kharkov were men. The sense of a common humanity only seldom touches Simone de Beauvoir; when it does, she writhes in anguish. Her inability to relate to people with whom she is not intimate prevents her from feeling for them. She is prevented from exposure to reality by the words she has previously chosen to describe that reality. (p. 69)

If Marks were simply trying to argue against the death penalty, I would certainly support her as against Beauvoir. True to her abstract humanist commitment, however, Marks does not raise such concrete political concerns. Her point is not only that we ought to *feel for* the death of Hitler and Mussolini, but that Beauvoir betrays her lack of humanity (the *topos* of the cold and uncaring political woman) in refusing to do so in 1946.

The priggish schoolgirl: irony as a rhetoric of hostility

Not surprisingly, the most important *topos* used to disparage Beauvoir, an outspoken woman and a highly qualified teacher of philosophy, is that of the bluestocking. Insisting on the cold, dry, desexualized nature of the intellectual woman, this figure tends to merge with that of the *unfeminine* or *non-maternal* woman studied above. Thus Konrad Bieber is astonished to discover that when Beauvoir found herself cooking meals for Sartre and their friends during the war, the food actually turned out to be edible: 'The idea of this reputed bluestocking cooking meals that found approval, in a hotel room, on make-shift ranges is not without its spice', he exclaims (p. 64).

One of the most fascinating exploitations of the *topos* is to be found in a lengthy article on Beauvoir published in the Rouen newspaper *Paris-Normandie* in 1954. Entitled 'Simone de Beauvoir – "popess" of existentialism' the report purports to be reproducing some diary notes jotted down by one of Beauvoir's students at the *lycée* Jeanne d'Arc in Rouen in 1934. The student remains unidentified, and the authenticity of this 'diary' strikes me as extremely dubious. Whether fiction or fact, however, this piece of journalism provides an excellent illustration of the way a provincial French newspaper in 1954 saw fit to present an internationally known female intellectual.

More than two-thirds of the purported diary excerpts are taken up with detailed descriptions of Beauvoir's physical attributes. The first impression is of a relatively plain being who lacks balance: 'The teacher, Mlle de Beauvoir, walks with mincing steps, as if she might lose her balance at any moment. . . . I look at her: she is a small, very young and pleasant woman, but she is not pretty.' After some detailed descriptions of her face and head, the student concludes that there are two really remarkable things about this woman: 'Two things hold one's attention: the temples and the veins on the neck. When she talks, they swell up and throb, revealing an intense intellectual activity.' Having thus transferred the phallus to the thinking woman's head, the student logically enough goes on to declare it missing elsewhere: 'The rest of this childish body is not harmonious. When she stands up, she seems out of balance', she writes. 'One has the impression that something is lacking.'[18] The teacher's body, it would seem, is neither female nor male, but childish, or in other words lacking not only in phallic power, but in any kind of adult sexuality.

An interesting variation on the cliché of the bluestocking is the *topos* of the priggish schoolgirl or the stuffy schoolmarm. In the French context, the explicit references to the *school* situation has a series of quite specific implications. This is not simply a general dismissal of women's pathetic efforts to appear as learned as men are. What really irks Beauvoir's critics, and particularly the French ones, is the fact that she is an intellectual woman whose formal training and qualifications more often than not outshine their own. In a review of *The Prime of Life* from 1961, René Girard uses the figure of the schoolgirl to great effect:

Early in life, Mlle de Beauvoir was one of those little female prodigies who win all the prizes in school and get the *mentions très bien*, thus poisoning the lives of their more relaxed brothers and cousins. These female prodigies are one of the truly national institutions of France. Academic achievements of children are a major field of competition between families of the middle class. The girls are usually ahead of the boys because they are more eager to please their fathers. Immediately after the *baccalauréat*, however, they are expected to abandon all intellectual pursuits in order to become wives and mothers. Competition is suddenly shifted to other fields. Little geniuses with their heads full of trigonometry and Kantian philosophy are often seen never to open another book for the rest of their lives.

Being a particularly brilliant subject, Mme de Beauvoir could not stand the thought of forsaking the *mention très bien*, and she simply refused to be reconverted to home life, thus manifesting for the first time that spirit of rebellion which made her famous and which is still alive in her. However much we admire this valorous feat, we

must not exaggerate the scope of the revolution. . . . Mme
de Beauvoir is the voice of all the other feminine first prize
winners. (p. 85)

Girard brilliantly conveys the meaning of the *topos*:
schoolboys are relaxed and easy going; schoolgirls are swots
and killjoys, turning their brothers into mere also-rans,
not because they are more intelligent, but because they
overwork in order to please their fathers. Schoolgirls,
moreover, are never true intellectuals: as soon as they come
first in the all-female competition for the only important
first prize in life – a man – they are only too happy never
to touch a book again.

In France, journalists and reviewers in popular magazines
and newspapers are particularly fond of this figure. Ranging
from mere quips ('Simone de Beauvoir or the teaching
body'[19]) to spiteful obituaries ('Une épouvantable donneuse
de leçons' – 'a dreadful teacher of lessons'),[20] the *topos* is
wheeled out whenever Beauvoir's ideas are to be dismissed.
'Her memoirs are very neatly [*très sagement*] organised
around certain themes', Mathieu Galey (1972) writes in
his review of *All Said and Done*, 'the dissertation is well
constructed.' 'One has the impression . . . of listening to
a lecture *ex cathedra*', *Le Monde* complains after seeing
Beauvoir on television.[21] Occasionally, the figure turns up
in reverse: how surprising that Beauvoir is *not* a ferocious
bluestocking! In a well-intentioned review of *Memoirs of a
Dutiful Daughter*, Geneviève Gennari exclaims: 'And it is
not a *monstre sacré*, a Minerva sprung fully armed from
the brains of the god of philosophy, or perhaps emerged
by spontaneous generation, that we meet!'.

Schoolgirls and schoolmarms are desexualized (the dried-
up spinster and old maid are not far away), rigid, predictable
and *confined* in their knowledge; true intellectuals are
virile, wide-ranging, supple and inventive. School suits
women because it is the place for serious and disciplined
submission to the *doxa*; real intellectual creativity, however,

is playful, unpredictable and transgressive, and as such necessarily male. If Beauvoir quickly earnt a reputation for 'courageous effort, prodigious research and straightforward habits of thought', as Mary Ellmann once put it ('The Dutiful', p. 94), this is not altogether as flattering as it may sound.

Much in evidence throughout Beauvoir criticism, the sarcasm and irony that Elaine Marks comments on is nowhere more apparent than in the frequent attacks on the pretensions of the intellectual woman. It should be remembered, however, that the generalized use of the personality *topos*, which seeks to displace interest away from the woman's thoughts and on to her body or character, also has deeply anti-intellectual effects. Among critics who are out to disparage Beauvoir as an intellectual, one of the most frequent terms of abuse is *naïvety*. The combination of irony with the accusation of naïvety, I would argue, is not a coincidence. Rhetorically, classical irony signals above all *distance* and *superiority*. As a highly successful intellectual woman Beauvoir is deeply threatening to insecure males with academic or journalistic pretensions: as René Girard shows, she simply refuses to leave the intellectual race to the men. Through the use of irony, the critic manages at once to situate himself at a safe distance from his female challenger, and to signal his own subtle superiority of insight.

Classical irony relies for its effect on the assumption of a clear-cut opposition between appearances and truth: the ironist is presumed to have true insight; his victim to be blinded by ignorance. It can be shown that such irony works by appealing to a set of values assumed to be shared by the ironist and her audience.[22] If this process fails, the irony disappears. This, incidentally, is why the patriarchal irony liberally bestowed on Beauvoir is so galling to feminists. In a political context such use of irony reproduces the opposition between ideology and empirical truth discussed above. By relying on the implicit assumption of common standards, irony also represses the need for explicit confrontation of opposing world-views. Deeply aggressive, however, classical irony reproduces the triangular structure of victimization that Freud finds at work in jokes and witticisms (*Jokes and Their Relations to the Unconscious* chapter V). For the irony to work there must be complicity between the ironist and the 'ironee', a complicity where both take their superiority over the 'ironized' for granted. As one of the aims of the irony is to produce maximal distance between the values and insights of the ironist and her victim, the 'ironized' victim tends to come across as the embodiment of whatever is taken to be the direct opposite of the ironist's own standards.

The opposite of irony is naïvety: what could be more distant from the rhetorical elegance of irony than the artless and childish lack of discrimination of the naïve? The figure of irony, then, is deeply epistemological: what is to be distinguished is knowledge and ignorance, insight and blindness. This, I think, accounts for the frequency and prevalence of the use of sarcasm and irony in Beauvoir criticism. Nothing can be more *ironic* than to attack an intellectual, a teacher of philosophy, a writer of philosophical and political essays for her *ignorance*. By working the naïvety *topos* to exhaustion, her critics want to convey a picture of a childlike creature, unconscious of the effects of her own discourse. As such this figure rejoins and reinforces that of the schoolgirl: both work together to produce the image of a *false intellectual*. That it is a woman who is denounced as an epistemological impostor in this way is precisely the point: women's right to intellectual activity – and particularly to philosophy – has always been hotly contested by patriarchal ideology. Simone de Beauvoir's fate at the hands of her critics shows that the struggle is by no means over today.

NOTES

I am grateful to Penny Boumelha for her comments on an earlier version of this paper.

A note on the text Documentation referring to the list of works cited is provided in the text. In some cases, however, where such documentation would make the text too cumbersome to read, notes have been used. Whenever the reference given is to a French text, the translation is mine. Whenever possible, I supply two page references to texts by Simone de Beauvoir: the first is to the published English translation and the second to the French original; both editions used are listed under 'References'. References to newspaper and magazine articles do not always contain page numbers since many of the archives and *dossiers* consulted do not consistently provide them.

1 Drawing on magazine and newspaper articles as well as academic research, I do not limit myself to criticism in the academic sense. In this chapter, in order to avoid awkward repetitions, I sometimes use the term 'criticism' as a near-synonym to 'reception'.
2 For Benveniste, all actual use of language is a discursive act of *énonciation*. The act of enunciation produces the discourse as discourse. I would add that the *énonciation* necessarily intervenes in a real historical and social space, and that there is no need to theorize the speaking subject as a bodyless, transcendental ego, as Benveniste himself does. Every *énonciation* produces a statement, an *énoncé*, or in other words: what is actually being said. The *énoncé* is not simply the 'contents' of the statement: it is the material structure of signifiers produced by the act of *énonciation*. See Benveniste, 'Les relations de temps' and 'L'appareil formel'.
3 Keefe is an exception to this rule.
4 In my own reading of full-length studies on Beauvoir published in French or English from 1958 to 1988 I found it useful to divide my material in the following rough groups (I have included the year of original publication in order to help the reader identify the emergence and disappearance of the various trends):

Catholic   Henry (1961), Hourdin (1962), Gagnebin (1968).
Existentialist/Socialist   Jeanson (1966), Julienne-Caffié (1966).
Scholarly   Gennari (1958), Berghe (1966), Jaccard (1968), Lasocki (1971), Moubachir (1972), Cayron (1972), Marks (1973), Cottrell (1975), Audet (1979), Bieber (1979), Whitmarsh (1981), Keefe (1983), Marks (ed.) (1987).
Popular   Descubes (1974), Madsen (1977), Armogathe (1977), Francis and Niepce (1978), Gonthier and Francis (1985), Eaubonne (1986), Appignanesi (1988), Winegarten (1988).
Feminist   Lilar (1969), Leighton (1975), Ascher (1981), Zéphir (1982), Hatcher (1984), Evans (1985), Okeley (1986), Fallaize (1988).

These categories are fairly rough and ready. The division between 'scholarly' and 'popular' is particularly impressionistic. This list does not encompass books where important chapters or sections are devoted to Beauvoir. I would nevertheless like to mention Nahas (1957) as an important early study partly devoted to Beauvoir. I also consulted Barnes (1961), Fitch (1964), Huvos (1972) and Celeux (1986), all highly scholarly works containing one or more chapters on Beauvoir. A pioneering feminist study is Ophir (1976), which contains a systematic reading of Beauvoir's *The Woman Destroyed*. Evans (1987) and Sankovich (1988) also contain feminist readings of Beauvoir.

5 'Jeune fille de la ville, simple et frivole.' The example which follows is: 'Goûts, lectures de midinette'.
6 He has competition, however. The obituary in *Minute* after Beauvoir's and Genet's death was entitled 'Deux morts sans importance' ('Two deaths of no importance'), and concluded that now that they are dead, 'this world seems a little bit cleaner [*un peu plus propre*] to us'.
7 Eric Neuhoff, 'Jean-Paul, Tintin et Milou'.
8 Etienne Lalou, 'La raison n'a pas toujours raison', p. 108.
9 Bernard Pivot, 'Simone de Beauvoir: une vraie femme de lettres (pour le courrier du coeur)', p. 29.
10 The great exception here is Francis Jeanson's study of her memoirs where he brilliantly demonstrates the way in which serious philosophical concerns underpin the text.

11 Julien Cheverny, 'Une bourgeoise modèle'.
12 Claude Jannoud, 'L'oeuvre: une vulgarisation plus qu'une création'.
13 Michèle Levaux, 'Simone de Beauvoir: une féministe exceptionnelle', p. 494.
14 It does happen, however. In his *Croquis de mémoire*, Sartre's ex-secretary, Jean Cau, claims that: '"The milk of human kindness" is not only undrinkable, but unknown to him. If he swallowed as much as a mouthful of it, he would think he was taking a drug. He would no longer be, and I'll pronounce the word, *free*' (p. 251).
15 Winegarten, never strong on facts, does not give the actual figures. For Sartre, see Cohen-Solal p. 663; for Beauvoir, Francis and Gonthier (English trans.) p. 362.
16 Quoted from the manuscript version of chapter 1.
17 The last sentence is awkward to translate. The original reads: 'Et cette oeuvre d'une ambition toute masculine suscite plus de curiosité qu'elle n'exerce d'influence vraie.'
18 All references from Reuillard. Unfortunately page numbers were not provided on the cuttings in the Bibliothèque Marguerite Durand.
19 'Simone de Beauvoir ou le corps enseignant.' Attributed to François Nourrissier in an anonymous and untitled notice in *Carrefour*, 24 April 1957.
20 Jacques Henric, 'Pourquoi ces biographies aseptisées?'
21 Claude Sarraute, 'Féminisme = humanisme', p. 11.
22 I am indebted to Culler's discussion of irony in his *Flaubert*, pp. 185–207.

REFERENCES

Appignanesi, Lisa, *Simone de Beauvoir* (Harmondsworth, Middx.: Penguin, 1988).
Armogathe, Daniel, *Le Deuxième sexe: Simone de Beauvoir* (Paris: Hatier, 1977).
Ascher, Carol, *Simone de Beauvoir: A Life of Freedom* (Brighton: Harvester, 1981).

Audet, Jean-Raymond, *Simone de Beauvoir face à la mort* (Lausanne: L'Age d'homme, 1979).

Barnes, Hazel A. *The Literature of Possibility: A Study in Humanist Existentialism* (London: Tavistock, 1961).

Beauvoir, Simone de, 'Oeil pour oeil', *L'Existentialisme et la sagesse des nations* (Paris: Nagel, 1948) pp. 125–64.

Beauvoir, Simone de, *Mémoires d'une jeune fille rangée*, Coll. Folio (Paris: Gallimard, 1958). Trans. James Kirkup, *Memoirs of a Dutiful Daughter*, 1959 (Harmondsworth, Middx.: Penguin, 1987).

Beauvoir, Simone de, *Une mort très douce*. Coll. Folio (Paris: Gallimard, 1964). Trans. Patrick O'Brian, *A Very Easy Death*, 1966 (Harmondsworth, Middx.: Penguin, 1983).

Beauvoir, Simone de, *Le Sang des autres*. Coll. Folio (Paris: Gallimard, 1945). Trans. Yvonne Moyse and Roger Senhouse, *Blood of Others*, 1948 (Harmondsworth, Middx.: Penguin, 1964).

Beauvoir, Simone de, *Tout compte fait*. Coll. Folio (Paris: Gallimard, 1972). Trans. Patrick O'Brian, *All Said and Done*, 1974 (Harmondsworth, Middx.: Penguin, 1987).

Benveniste, Emile, 'Les relations de temps dans le verbe français', *Problèmes de linguistique générale*, vol. 1, Coll. Tel. (Paris: Gallimard, 1966) pp. 237–50.

Benveniste, Emile, 'L'appareil formel de l'énonciation'. *Problèmes de linguistique générale*, vol. 2, Coll. Tel. (Paris: Gallimard, 1966) pp. 79–88.

Berghe, Chr. L van der, *Dictionnaire des idées dans l'oeuvre de Simone de Beauvoir* (The Hague: Mouton, 1966).

Bieber, Konrad, *Simone de Beauvoir* (Boston: Twayne, 1972).

Boisdeffre, Pierre de, *Une histoire vivante de la littérature d'aujourd'hui, 1938–58* (Paris: Le livre contemporain, 1958).

Bourdoiseau, Yannick, 'Sous les couvertures', *Minute*, 25 April 1986.

Cambell, James, 'Experiencing Egoism', review of *The Tongue Set Free*, by Elias Canetti, *The Times Literary Supplement*, 26 August 1988, p. 926.

Carrefour, 24 October 1957.

Cau, Jean, *Croquis de mémoire* (Paris: Julliard, 1985).

Cayron, Claire, *La nature chez Simone de Beauvoir* (Paris: Gallimard, 1973).

Celeux, Anne-Marie, *Jean-Paul Sartre, Simone de Beauvoir: Une expérience commune, deux écritures* (Paris: Nizet, 1986).

Chaigne, Louis, 'Simone de Beauvoir: Prix Goncourt', *Le Courrier français*, 11 November 1954.

Cheverny, Julien, 'Une bourgeoise modèle: Simone de Beauvoir', *Figaro Magazine*, 17 February 1979, p. 57.

Chrestien, Michel, Review of *La Force des choses*, *La Nation française*, 13 November 1963. See Julienne-Caffié, pp. 229–30.

Cohen-Solal, Annie, *Sartre 1905–1980* (Paris: Gallimard, 1985).

Cottrell, Robert, *Simone de Beauvoir* (New York: Ungar, 1975).

Culler, Jonathan, *Flaubert: The Uses of Uncertainty* (London: Elek, 1974).

Descubes, Madeleine, *Connaître Simone de Beauvoir* (Paris: Resma, 1974).

'Deux morts sans importance', *Minute*, 18 April 1986.

Domaize, Pierre, Review of *La Force des choses*, *La Nation française*, 30 January 1964. See Julienne-Caffié, p. 233.

Eagleton, Terry, *Ideology*, (London: Verso) forthcoming.

Ellmann, Mary, 'The Dutiful Simone de Beauvoir', in Marks, *Critical Essays* pp. 94–101.

Ellmann, Mary, *Thinking About Women* (New York: Harcourt, 1968).

Evans, Martha Noel, *Masks of Tradition: Women and the Politics of Writing in Twentieth Century France* (Ithaca, NY: Cornell University Press, 1987).

Eaubonne, Françoise d', *Une femme nommée Castor: Mon amie Simone de Beauvoir* (Paris: Encre, 1986).

Evans, Mary, *Simone de Beauvoir: A Feminist Mandarin* (London: Tavistock, 1985).

Fallaize, Elizabeth, *The Novels of Simone de Beauvoir* (London: Routledge, 1988).

Fitch, Brian T., *Le sentiment d'étrangeté chez Malraux, Sartre, Camus et Simone de Beauvoir* (Paris: Minard, 1964).

Fouque, Antoinette, Interview, *Libération*, 15 April 1986, p. 5.

Francis, Claude and Gonthier, Fernande, *Simone de Beauvoir*, trans. Lisa Nesselson (London: Sidgwick, 1987).

Francis, Claude and Niepce, Janine, *Simone de Beauvoir et le cours du monde* (Paris: Klincksieck, 1978).

Freud, Sigmund, *The Interpretation of Dreams*, 1900, Pelican Freud Library 4 (Harmondsworth, Middx.: Penguin, 1976).

Freud, Sigmund, *Jokes and Their Relations to the Unconscious*, 1905, Pelican Freud Library 6 (Harmondsworth, Middx.: Penguin, 1983).

Gagnebin, Laurent, *Simone de Beauvoir ou le refus de l'indifférence* (Paris: Fischbacher, 1968).

Galey, Mathieu, 'Simone de Beauvoir: le temps vaincu', *L'Express*, 4 September 1972, pp. 87–8.

Gennari, Geneviève, *Simone de Beauvoir* (Paris: Ed. Universitaires, 1958).

Gennari, Geneviève, Review of *Mémoires d'une jeune fille rangée*, *Arts*, 8 October 1958.

Girard, René, 'Memoirs of a Dutiful Existentialist', in Marks, *Critical Essays* pp. 84–8.

Hatcher, Donald L., *Understanding 'The Second Sex'* (New York: Peter Lang, 1984).

Henric, Jacques, 'Pourquoi ces biographies aseptisées?' *Art Press*, vol. 104 (June 1986), p. 3.

Henry, A. M., *Simone de Beauvoir ou l'échec d'une chrétienté* (Paris: Fayard, 1961).

Hourdin, Georges, *Simone de Beauvoir et la liberté* (Paris: Cerf, 1962).

Huvos, Kornel, *Cinq mirages américains* (Paris: Didier, 1972).

Jaccard, Annie-Claire, *Simone de Beauvoir* (Zürich: Juris Druck, 1968).

Jannoud, Claude. 'L'oeuvre: une vulgarisation plus qu'une création', *Le Monde*, 15 April 1986.

Jeanson, Francis, *Simone de Beauvoir ou l'entreprise de vivre* (Paris: Seuil, 1966).

Julienne-Caffié, Serge, *Simone de Beauvoir* (Paris: Gallimard, 1966).

Keefe, Terry, *Simone de Beauvoir: A Study of her Writings* (London: Harrap, 1983).

Lalou, Etienne, 'La raison n'a pas toujours raison', *L'Express*, 12 December 1966, p. 107–8.

Lasocki, Anne-Marie, *Simone de Beauvoir ou l'entreprise d'écrire: Essai de commentaire par les textes* (The Hague: Nijhoff, 1970).

Le Doeuff, Michèle, 'Simone de Beauvoir and Existentialism', *Feminist Studies*, vol. 6 (Summer 1980), pp. 277–89.

Le Doeuff, Michèle, 'Sartre: L'Unique Sujet parlant', *Esprit*,

May 1984, pp. 181–91.

Le Doeuff, Michèle *L'étude et le rouet: des femmes, de la philosophie etc.* (Paris: Seuil, 1989).

Leighton, Jean, *Simone de Beauvoir on Woman* (Rutherford: Fairleigh Dickinson, 1975).

Levaux, Michèle, 'Simone de Beauvoir, une féministe exceptionelle', *Études*, April 1984, pp. 493–8.

Lévi-Strauss, Claude, *Tristes tropiques* (Paris: Plon, 1955).

Lilar, Suzanne, *Le malentendu du Deuxième sexe* (Paris: PUF, 1969).

Madsen, Axel, *Hearts and Minds: The Common Journey of Simone de Beauvoir and Jean-Paul Sartre* (New York: Morrow, 1977).

Marks, Elaine, *Simone de Beauvoir: Encounters with Death* (New Brunswick, NJ: Rutgers University Press, 1973).

Marks, Elaine, (ed.) *Critical Essays on Simone de Beauvoir* (Boston: Hall, 1987).

Marks, Elaine, 'Transgressing the (In)cont(in)ent Boundaries: The Body in Decline', *Yale French Studies*, vol. 72 (1987), pp. 181–200.

Moubachir, Chantal, *Simone de Beauvoir* (Paris: Seghers, 1981).

Nahas, Hélène, *La femme dans la littérature existentielle* (Paris: PUF, 1957).

Neuhoff, Eric, 'Jean-Paul, Tintin et Milou', *Le Quotidien de Paris*, 14 December 1981.

Okeley, Judith, *Simone de Beauvoir* (London: Virago, 1986).

Ophir, Anne, *Regards féminins: Beauvoir/Etcherelli/Rochefort. Condition féminine et création littéraire* (Paris: Denoël/Gonthier, 1976).

Pivot, Bernard, 'Simone de Beauvoir: une vraie femme de lettres (pour le courrier du coeur)', *Figaro littéraire*, 30 October 1967, p. 29.

Poulet, Robert, *La lanterne magique* (Paris: Debresse, 1956).

Reuillard, Gabriel, 'Simone de Beauvoir – "papesse" de l'existentialisme', *Paris-Normandie*, 17 February 1954.

Sankovitch, Tilde A., *French Women Writers and the Book: Myths of Access and Desire* (Syracuse, NY: Syracuse University Press, 1988).

Sarraute, Claude, 'Féminisme = humanisme', *Le Monde*, 6–7 April 1975, p. 11.

Senart, Philippe, Review of *La force des choses*, *La table ronde*,

December 1963. See Julienne-Caffié, pp. 231–2.

Whitmarsh, Anne, *Simone de Beauvoir and the Limits of Commitment* (Cambridge: Cambridge University Press, 1981).

Winegarten, Renée, *Simone de Beauvoir: A Critical View* (Oxford: Berg, 1988).

Zéphir, Jacques J., *Le néo-féminisme de Simone de Beauvoir: trente ans après Le deuxième sexe: un post-scriptum* (Paris: Denoël/Gonthier, 1982).

Intentions and Effects: Rhetoric and Identification in Simone de Beauvoir's 'The Woman Destroyed'

Simone de Beauvoir's short story 'The Woman Destroyed',[1] first published in January 1968, is one of her most popular texts.[2] Neither as intellectually complex as *She Came to Stay* (1943), nor as politically challenging as *The Mandarins* (1954), it is not among her most important literary works. It does, however, have the distinction of being the most persistently misunderstood, at least according to Beauvoir herself. In *All Said and Done* (*ASD*, 1972), the fourth volume of her autobiography, she writes that when it was first published, the great majority of her female readers persisted in identifying with the heroine, Monique, whereas she had intended to portray her as a woman victimized by her own delusions, perversely refusing freedom and responsibility in the face of reason. My own experience of teaching the text tends to confirm Beauvoir's impression: most of my students flatly reject the 'authorial' reading, take the unfaithful husband, Maurice, to be the scoundrel and identify with the protagonist. Consequently they refuse to read the end of the story simply as bleak and despondent, insisting instead that it somehow *must* represent a new departure for Monique. The question I would like to address here is *why* this text provokes such persistent 'misreadings'. What rhetorical strategies contribute to produce such a conflict of interpretations? And why does the conflict turn on the question of sympathy or identification?

These questions raise the difficult problem of intentionality in literary texts. Without wanting to rehearse here the various arguments advanced on this issue, I think it is necessary to distinguish between the author's declared intentions on the one hand, and what one might want to call the intentionality of the text on the other, which I see as the 'logic' of the text as produced by the reader, or in other words the feeling that *this* is what the various elements studied are structured to add up to, whether the author knows it or not. In this paper I also sometimes use the term 'authorial reading' by which I understand an effort to read the text according to the author's own explicit intentions or comments. Needless to say I am not assuming that the author's intentions always allow for such an 'authorial reading': it will always be necessary to *show*, not simply to assume, that a plausible reading can in fact be derived from such a statement of intent. The implication is that, in principle at least, an explicit authorial intention need not have any discernible textual effects at all. In this paper, then, I will first examine Beauvoir's stated intentions, and then try to produce an 'authorial reading' based on it. Given the determined disagreement between the author and many of her readers on this score, I will also try to show that this particular short story generates a series of other textual effects (to do with language, meaning and epistemology) which necessarily undermine the authorial reading. Finally, I examine the way in which the formal strategies of the text produce an impossible position for the reader, one in which she can only choose one perspective at the cost of blinding herself to another.

Before turning to these issues, I should say that I use the word 'author' and the name Simone de Beauvoir as synonymous with the 'speaking (or writing) subject' or the 'subject of the enunciation', in Kristeva's and Benveniste's sense of these terms.[3] Thus the female protagonist, Monique, is simultaneously part of the text of Beauvoir's *énoncé*, and the subject of her own act of enunciation, which is the writing of her diary. As such, Monique is at once a double of Beauvoir – another writing subject – and simply an effect of her discourse.

The existentialist reading

Simone de Beauvoir's own reading is entirely plausible, thoroughly consistent as it is with her own existentialist positions and her analysis of the female condition in *The Second Sex* (1949). In *All Said and Done*, Beauvoir claims that she has never written a more depressing piece of fiction than 'The Woman Destroyed':

> I have never written anything more sombre than 'The Woman Destroyed': the whole of the second part is one long cry of agony, and the final crumbling of the heroine is sadder than death itself. (*ASD*, p. 142/178, trans. amended)[4]

The fact that the story appeared in instalments in *Elle* before publication, brought Beauvoir hundreds of thousands of new readers. They reacted passionately to the text. Beauvoir comments:

> Immediately I was overwhelmed with letters from women, destroyed, half-destroyed or in the act of being destroyed. They identified themselves with the heroine; they attributed all possible virtues to her and they were astonished that she should remain attached to a man so unworthy of her. Their partiality made it evident that as far as their husbands, their rivals and they themselves were concerned, they shared Monique's blindness. Their reactions were based

upon an immense incomprehension [*un énorme contre-sens*]. (*ASD*, p. 142/177–8)

It is interesting – and somewhat puzzling – to note that the reactions of the readers of *Elle* in 1967 closely correspond to those of my own (and many of my colleagues') students in the late 1980s. Thus the advent of the women's movement would seem to have made no difference at all to this specific reading position. In 1967 and 1968, the critics in general disliked the book. According to Beauvoir, one of them, Bernard Pivot, even claimed that 'since "The Woman Destroyed" was appearing in a women's magazine it was therefore a shop-girl's romance with pink bows on it' (*ASD*, 142/178).[5] On the whole Beauvoir did not take such criticisms and 'misreadings' seriously. But when some feminists objected that these stories had nothing militant about them, she was more affected, although not to the point of actually agreeing with them:

'She has betrayed us!' they cried; and they sent me reproachful letters. There is no reason at all why one should not draw a feminist conclusion from 'The Woman Destroyed': Monique's unhappiness arose from her having agreed to be dependent. But I really do not feel obliged to choose exemplary heroines. It does not seem to me that describing failure, error and bad faith means betraying anyone at all. (pp. 143–4/179)

But how did Beauvoir come to write such a gloomy story? Her own explanation is that the material came from her female friends and acquaintances. Around 1966, she tells us, several women in their forties confided in her their disarray at losing their husband to another woman. In spite of the considerable differences between these women, they had one thing in common:

The women could not even remotely understand what was happening to them; they thought their husband's behaviour contradictory, abnormal and deviant, and the rival unworthy of his love: their world was falling to pieces and they ended up by no longer knowing who they were. (p. 140/175)

In a striking turn of phrase Beauvoir goes on to say: 'L'idée m'est venue de donner à voir leur nuit' (p. 175), which literally means that she wanted to 'make their night visible', and which Patrick O'Brian translates as: 'I had the idea of speaking about their darkness and making it evident' (p. 140). Here the story is presented as at once true and distant: as a problem that affects *other* women, not Simone de Beauvoir. Attributing a position of discursive and epistemological superiority to herself, Beauvoir seems to be insisting that *she* can expose the plight of these women precisely because she is not in the grip of their illusions. But perhaps she protests too much here? Is there not a whiff of denegation about this attempt to ascribe the problem of jealousy and loss of love to other and younger women? (Her informants are 'in their forties', whereas Beauvoir herself was 58 in 1966.) This suspicion is reinforced if one stops to consider that 'The Woman Destroyed' is only the last in a series of texts in which Beauvoir chooses to focus on the plight of a jealous woman. Many critics have been quick to point out that while female jealousy is surprisingly absent from Beauvoir's autobiography, it features often and insistently in her fiction and essays. Thus both her first published novel, *She Came to Stay*, and her last work of fiction, 'The Woman Destroyed', feature a female protagonist suffering agonies of jealousy. Jealousy is also discussed in some detail in *The Second Sex* and passionately exposed in the tragic case of Paule in *The Mandarins*. And Murielle, the cruel, paranoid and narcissistic protagonist of the short story 'Monologue' (in *The Woman Destroyed*) can be read as at once a more obsessive version of Paule and a sadistic illustration of the narcissistic woman in love as described in *The Second Sex*.

The fact that Beauvoir here comes across as somewhat disingenuous and certainly as condescending, does not give us *carte blanche* to ignore her ostensible intentions. If she expresses her desire to expose other women's ignorance, it is overwhelmingly probable that it is because she wants to change the situation that brings it about. The language she uses ('reveal', 'make visible') is very similar to that of Sartre in his 1948 essay *What is Literature?* And as late as 1964, in the great debate between *nouveaux romanciers* and existentialists on commitment in literature, Beauvoir still defended engagement in much the same terms as those first used by Sartre in 1948.[6] For Sartre and Beauvoir, to disclose or reveal (*dévoiler*) the world is to act on it:

> Thus, by speaking, I reveal the situation by my very intention of changing it; I reveal it to myself and to others in order to change it. I strike at its very heart, I transfix it, and I display it in full view; at present I dispose of it; with every word I utter I involve myself a little more in the world. (*What is Literature?* p. 13)

But Sartre's language here is not only a plea for engagement in literature, it is also – or first and foremost – a display of discursive power. In the two sentences quoted here, he manages to squeeze in no less than seven 'I' and three 'my' or 'myself', which is no little feat in itself. On the other hand, the modest 'and to others' is not repeated once, and consequently reads like a hurried afterthought, not as the very *raison d'être* of the writer's commitment. On this evidence, the politically engaged writer is at least as involved with his own prowess, his own capacity to reveal the truth (*I* reveal, *I* strike, *I* transfix, *I* display . . .), as with his political message. In the same way Beauvoir's genuine commitment to change is structured through a discursive position that signals power, superior insight and a hierarchical mode of thought.

Implicitly, Beauvoir's autobiography displays the same emphasis on the superiority of the writer. Here every single text published by Beauvoir receives its own authorial interpretation: the autobiography becomes a repertoire of *authorized* readings, a series of efforts to enforce the law, or in other words, to *police* the reading of her own texts. On the whole she has been remarkably successful in this operation: to my knowledge very few critics indeed have set out – deliberately or not – to subvert her views. But there is of course also a sense in which the very intensity of Beauvoir's efforts to enforce the true meaning of her texts may make the sceptical reader wonder why she protests so much. Perhaps there is something in these texts that threatens to escape even Simone de Beauvoir?

The politics of Beauvoir's discursive enterprise is ambiguous: as we have seen, she herself claims that the story is compatible with feminist politics, but that is on two conditions only: firstly, that we accept her own interpretation, that is, that Monique is the author of her own downfall; and secondly, that we agree that the best feminist reading available is to turn Monique's tale into a terrible warning to others. A feminist who balks at submitting to so much authorial authority will surely be cast out among the 'partial', 'blind' and 'incomprehending' readers of *Elle*.

This impression of discursive superiority is reinforced by Beauvoir's account of the structure of her short story. She finds Monique guilty of an unexpiable crime: that of seeking to escape from the truth (see *ASD*, p. 140/175). In order to emphasize this point, she claims, she deliberately structured the narrative like a detective story, packing the text with clues pointing to the real author of the crime. Whereas Monique wants to make us believe that the scoundrel is Maurice, or possibly the evil rival Noëllie, Beauvoir points the finger at Monique herself. Her language signals the intensity of her engagement when Beauvoir sets out clinically and methodically to construct a veritable witch-hunt in which to trap her protagonist:

> The whole of Monique's efforts tend to obscure [the light]; from one page to another her diary contradicts itself – but it does so through fresh omissions and new falsehoods. She herself weaves the darkness in which she sinks far down, so far that she loses her own image. I hoped that people would read the book as a detective-story; here and there I scattered clues that would allow the reader to find the key to the mystery – but only if he tracked Monique as one tracks down the guilty character [*à condition qu'on dépiste Monique comme on dépiste un coupable*]. (p. 140/175–6)

The repository of truth in the story is not Monique, but Maurice, Beauvoir claims: 'Intellectually the husband is her superior by far and he has long since stopped loving her' (p. 140/175). It may not be intentional, but she does make this sound rather as if the latter was a necessary consequence of the former. However that may be, the reader now has a clear recipe for how to read the story: accept everything Maurice says, particularly when he is angry, and the truth will be clear. Since such an estimable man likes her – even loves her – the independent career-woman Noëllie must be an excellent character, the dependent housewife Monique simply possessive and ignorant. For most readers, whether or not they otherwise agree with the author, the fact that Maurice has managed to lie to Monique about his affairs with other women for over eight years makes this interpretation somewhat uncomfortable. Curiously enough his commonplace and petty avoidance of the sexual truth is not supposed to cast a shadow over his heroic status in his author's eyes, nor is it supposed to prevent him from representing reason and the intellect in the text. In this sense, at least, there is more than one parallel between the representation of Maurice in this short story and the representation of Sartre in Beauvoir's memoirs and in the *Lettres au Castor*.

From an existentialist perspective, Monique has made a series of crucial errors. She is guilty of *mauvaise foi* (bad faith) in that she persists in denying her own freedom and therefore also her own responsibility for her life, choosing instead to define herself as a 'relative being'. Having defined herself entirely through her husband, Monique loses her own image when she loses him. Her definition of love is also cruelly flawed: she fails to realize that love is an active project, not a static essence. For Sartre and Beauvoir, to take the world as given (*donné*) is to deny freedom. The world is always already in process: every one of our actions transforms it, as it transforms us. If Maurice and Monique's interpretations of their marriage are radically opposed (see, for instance, the great scene between them on pp. 160–4/184–9), it is because he has changed through his struggle to realize his projects in the world, whereas she has remained faithful to a static image of herself, one originally reflected back to her by Maurice, but long since taken over by her and placed in some timeless realm outside history. In this sense he represents dynamism, activity and transcendence, whereas she represents immanence, passivity and inaction.

For an existentialist there is no such thing as a given, essential meaning of a situation. By choosing a project we shape our own identity, and create a position from which to interpret the world. But there is nothing inherent or necessary about this position or this project: it must always be renewed if it is to continue to define us. According to this view, if Monique slides helplessly from one interpretation to another, unable to get a grip on herself and the world, it is because her refusal to define herself through the recognition of her own freedom prevents her from forging a coherent position from which to perceive reality.

The fact that Monique gives up her own medical studies, and later refuses to take paid work, is crucial for the Beauvoirean reading of the story. Already in *The Second Sex* Beauvoir argued that economic liberation is the *sine qua non* of every other form of liberation. Her uncompromising message is clear: motherhood and marriage alone can never make a woman happy; paid work alone secures her independence. Monique is intended as a faithful illustration of this maxim.

To say that Monique derives her identity from her relationship with Maurice, is to say that when he no longer loves her, she is nobody. That she progressively loses her identity and slowly sinks into depression is a logical consequence of this position. For Monique, love made Maurice and her into a unity. They were each other, always and for ever. What she liked, he liked, and vice versa. Her constant use of 'we' indicates her incapacity to differentiate between them. Their very being is fixed once and for all in Monique's static image of their love. Maurice has no right to change: change can only signify falseness, lack of authenticity, superficiality or a lack of reality. In emphasizing the theme of unity between her and her husband (*on ne fait qu'un*), Monique repeats the mistake of Françoise in *She Came to Stay*. 'Harmony between two individuals is never a *donnée*, it must be worked for continually', Beauvoir writes in *The Prime of Life* (p. 260/ 299).

Monique's story also neatly illustrates Beauvoir's account of the dilemmas of the woman in love (*l'amoureuse*) in *The Second Sex*:

> It is, again, one of the loving woman's misfortunes to find that her very love disfigures her, destroys her; she is nothing more than this slave, this servant, this too ready mirror, this too faithful echo. When she becomes aware of this, her distress reduces her worth still further; in tears, demands and scenes she succeeds in losing all her attractiveness. An existent is what he does; but simply to be, she has come to rely on a consciousness not her own, and she has given up doing anything. (*The Second Sex*, p. 675/II.503)

But are there no mitigating circumstances? Even in *The Second Sex* Beauvoir takes pains to stress that it would be unfair to blame women for the negative and pathetic role they often come to play in patriarchal society: 'It is useless to apportion blame and excuses: justice can never be done in the midst of injustice' (p. 732/II.568). So why is she so determined to track Monique down like a criminal in this case? Already in 1947, two years before publishing *The Second Sex*, in *Pour une morale de l'ambiguïté*, she argues vigourously against blaming the victims of tyrannical regimes, such as slaves or the inmates of a harem, for their ignorance or indolence. But at the same time she stresses the necessity of seizing the very first opportunity of liberation:

Ignorance and error are facts as ineluctable as the walls of a prison. The black slave in the 18th century or the Muslim woman locked up in a harem do not have any tools which allow them to attack, be it only in thought or through astonishment or anger, the society which oppresses them. Their behaviour can only be defined and can only be judged from within this fact. It is possible that in their situation, which is limited as all human situations, they are already achieving a perfect affirmation of their freedom. But as soon as liberation appears as possible, not to take advantage of this possibility is to surrender one's freedom. This implies bad faith and is truly to be blamed [*une faute positive*]. (*Pour une morale*, p. 56)

If Monique is to be found guilty, it can only be because Simone de Beauvoir considered that by 1968 women had already gained their freedom. This is more than likely, since she argued the same thing as early as 1949: 'By and large we have won the game', she wrote in the introduction to *The Second Sex* (p. 27/I.29). On this view of post-war society, Monique has no excuses: neither a slave nor imprisoned in a harem, she is free to act. The implications are clear: to read the text in accordance with Beauvoir's intentions amounts to rejecting the need for any further social or institutional liberation of women. To argue with the readers of *Elle* that Monique is deserving of sympathy and support, and to make her an object of identification is at least implicitly to recognize that the victimization of women cannot simply be turned into a question of the individual woman's complicity or guilt. It also means emphasizing the responsibility of the husband where Beauvoir's own reading lets him off the hook rather too quickly, mostly on the grounds of his superior intelligence. It is no wonder that a reading which tends to exonerate philandering husbands and instead blames their unsuspecting wives for not being interesting enough failed to appeal to the readers of *Elle*. Finally, it is interesting to note that while Beauvoir soon came to recognize the error of her social and political analysis of women's position (she declared her support for the new feminist movement in a famous interview published in *Le Nouvel observateur* in 1972[7]), she apparently never changed her own reading of 'The Woman Destroyed'.

Jealousy, knowledge and language

Although the conflicting interpretations of the text now can be seen to have their roots in an implicit political disagreement over how to read women's position in society, there are other reasons why the Beauvoirean reading, for all its coherence, fails to satisfy most of her readers. There is, for instance, no analysis of formal effects. The fact that 'The Woman Destroyed' has the distinction of being the only fictional text by Beauvoir that foregrounds the writing process, and that the text itself is a first-person singular narrative, consisting of Monique's diary entries through a period of six and a half months (from 13 September to 24 March one year), is ignored. I shall return to the question of rhetorical and formal effects in the next section. There are nevertheless also a series of thematic and/or theoretical reasons why contemporary readers may fail to grasp Beauvoir's intentions. I now intend to examine three key issues here: the representation of jealousy and knowledge, and the implicit theory of language in 'The Woman Destroyed'.[8]

We have already seen that Beauvoir often returns to the theme of jealousy. Even more persistently, the question of knowledge haunts her texts. 'What is the truth – the truth about myself? about others? about the world?' is always the most pressing problem for her, whatever the genre she works in. For Beauvoir, knowledge represents control, power, self-confidence, self-reliance, solidity and energy. Lucidity, intelligence, rationality are key values in her textual universe. These are of course the very Cartesian values that exercise such powerful influence on French education and culture in general. If Monique at one point becomes obsessed with the question of whether she is intelligent, it is not only because she is a product of Simone de Beauvoir's imagination: it is also because she is French.[9] For Beauvoir, the theme of jealousy always involves that of knowledge,[10] and 'The Woman Destroyed' is no exception to this rule. The plot of the story casts Monique's breakdown as an effect of an increasingly frenzied quest for reliable knowledge. But jealousy breeds doubt, epistemological insecurity and an increasingly paranoid obsession with interpretation.[11]

From this perspective, the jealous subject is more like the detective than the criminal in a traditional thriller. This, surely, is another reason why the author's intentions go unnoticed: she has more or less unwittingly given Monique the role of quasi-paranoid reader of signs normally reserved for the detective. So how can the reader guess that she is in fact the culprit? Perceiving the world as a set of confusing clues to a hidden truth, Monique now desperately tries to endow every sign with a stable meaning. But unlike the detective story, jealousy offers no solutions: the very process of constant interpretation and reinterpretation ensures that the final closure of the thriller is not to be had. In the end, no evidence is final: everthing could always be interpreted differently. Othello's anguished plea for the 'proof, the ocular proof' is a plea for epistemological stability. But, as Monique knows, to the jealous subject visual evidence is no evidence at all: 'In any case, I should not have believed my eyes if I had seen him in bed with a woman' (p. 163/188, trans. amended). And Monique's efforts to trust other forms of knowledge – rumours, hearsay, graphology, even astrology – are shown to be vain as well as pathetic.

The first few entries in Monique's diary present us with what would seem to be firm epistemological ground. But an attentive reader will perceive the hollow note sounded already in the initial description of Les Salines. Looking at these eighteenth-century buildings, Monique thinks of their history and particularly of the fact that they never served any purpose: 'They are solid; they are real: yet their abandoned state changes them into a fantastic pretence [simulacre] – of what, one wonders' (p. 105/121). This evocation of a useless and somewhat empty semblance of a city hiding an unknown reality is not the product of an easy and relaxed mind, as Monique would like us – and herself – to think. Whether one sees this image as a deliberate and rather heavy-handed authorial metaphor of Monique's ignorance of her own situation, or as a first hint of the bleak final image in the book – that of the empty flat with the black windows and frightening doors behind which lurks the terrifying future (p. 220/252) – the salt works designed by Ledoux remain above all a monumental utopian project that failed.[12]

Monique's real or apparent peace of mind is soon

shattered by the news that her husband is having an affair with another woman, Noëllie Guérard. From this moment on the narrative becomes a chronicle of the slow and meticulous shattering of every illusion Monique ever had. Her illusions are relatively easy to catalogue, in spite of the fact that one set tends to spawn another with disconcerting speed. When jealousy hits her, Monique has cast herself once and for all as the devoted wife, housewife and mother and as *grande amoureuse* as well. Her immediate reaction is simply to construct her rival, Noëllie, as her own negative mirror image. To describe herself and 'the other woman', she resorts to a simple pattern of depth versus surface, essence versus contingence:

> One thing that helps me is that I am not physically jealous.
> . . . She [Noëllie] is the incarnation of everything we dislike – desire to succeed at any price, pretentiousness, love of money, a delight in display. She does not possess a single idea of her own; she is fundamentally devoid of sensitivity – she just goes along with the fashion. There is such barefacedness and exhibitionism in her capers with men that indeed I wonder whether she may not be frigid. (p. 120/138–9)

> But I am convinced of something that I cannot find adequate words for. With me Maurice has a relationship in depth, one to which his essential being is committed and which is therefore indestructible. He is only attached to Noëllie by his most superficial feelings – each of them might just as well be in love with someone else. Maurice and I are wholly conjoined. (p. 171/197)

If Monique is authentic (one of her favourite terms for herself, see for instance pp. 136/157 and 146/168), Noëllie must be false and superficial. If Monique is simple and natural, Noëllie must be a sophisticated snob. If Monique gave her daughters a good education, Noëllie must be destroying her own daughter, and so on. The equation works both ways: if Noëllie loves money, lacks originality and is a slave of fashion, it is the better to emphasize Monique's own sterling qualities. Monique's image of Noëllie is never corroborated by any other instance in the text, but neither is it contradicted: Maurice does not want to discuss her, and Monique's friends supply highly unreliable and contradictory information. So although the textual Noëllie comes across as nothing but the projection of Monique's hostility, the text surprisingly enough refrains from undercutting her account, and so comes to leave the question of Noëllie's 'real' nature fairly open.

As we have seen, Monique's sense of identity is bound up with her unshakeable belief in a fundamental unity between Maurice and herself. This belief cannot cope with the idea of difference. Monique therefore has to explain away the apparent difference in their interests and value judgements as an effect of ignorance, or more correctly, of incorrect knowledge. True knowledge, then, should theoretically help him to mend his ways:

> He is altogether gone from me if he likes being with someone I dislike so very much – and whom he ought to dislike if he were faithful to our code. Certainly he has altered. He lets himself be taken in by false values that we used to despise. Or he is simply completely mistaken about Noëllie. I wish the scales would drop from his eyes soon. (p. 136/157)

It is when Monique realizes that the 'superficial' or 'contingent' *historie de peau* (pp. 118/137, 122/140) that Maurice has with Noëllie is not simply an effect of ignorance, but real, that her whole epistemological system starts to break down. If she can no longer simply oppose surface to depth, false values to real values, Noëllie to herself, if the one set of terms surreptitiously starts to infect the other, chaos threatens to engulf her. Her 'saison en enfer' – the two weeks spent locked into her flat, dirty, drunk and desperate – express precisely this blurring of all categories.

Language and writing

As Monique grows increasingly jealous and desperate, references to the difficulties of writing, and particularly to the impossibility of seizing the truth in words, multiply. There is something paradoxical about the fact that Françoise, aspiring author and jealous protagonist of *She Came to Stay*, never utters a single reflection on the problems of language, whereas the crushed housewife of 'The Woman Destroyed' produces a running meta-commentary on questions of interpretation, communication and language, so that it is in 'The Woman Destroyed' and not *She Came to Stay* we find the most interesting reflections on the relationship between truth, knowledge and language.

Monique's writing is a doomed attempt to capture an essential identity through language. But writing, she soon realizes, is no ally in such a struggle. In fact, the very act of writing signals lack: lack of insight, lack of happiness, lack of stability:

> Yes, something has changed, since here I am writing about him, about myself, behind his back. If he had done so, I should have felt betrayed. Each of us used to be able to see entirely into the other. (p. 111/128–9)

Nor do words every convey reality, partly because writing always comes too late, *after* the event:

> Rages, nightmares, horror – words cannot encompass them. I set things down on paper when I recover strength, either in despair or in hope. But the feeling of total bewilderment, of stunned stupidity, of falling to pieces – these pages do not contain them. (p. 194/222, trans. amended)

Sometimes the writing subject lacks insight. Writing the truth as one sees it, is just another illusion: 'I was lying to myself. How I lied to myself!' (p. 194/223). Words are always open to reinterpretation; they offer no stability, no security. Rereading their old letters, Monique realizes that they now take on a different meaning from the one she thought they had, and earlier passages in her diary now strike her as false, wrong or deceitful. But the same process of rereading and reinterpretation may itself be repeated. Thus we are given five different versions of the moment when she waved goodbye to Maurice at the airport in Nice and four different views on the picnic in Les Salines or of the moment of Maurice's confession. So how can she trust her most recent 'insight'? What's true and what's false? And what can words do for us anyway?

It is on this point, I think, that Beauvoir's own and her present-day readers' interpretation differ most sharply. Beauvoir claims that one of the clues to Monique's guilt is the fact that she constantly contradicts herself, whereas 'post-modern' readers tend to see this confusion not as a sign of her stupidity or blindness but as an excellent illustration of the treacherous, deconstructive nature of *all* language. To the same readers, Monique's increasing epistemological helplessness does not necessarily signal her specific lack of insight, but rather a correct insight into the unstable nature of knowledge in general. In this way, 'The Woman Destroyed' may paradoxically – and quite unintentionally – come across as a far more 'modern' text than any of Beauvoir's other writings. There is also a sense in which 'The Woman Destroyed', precisely by emphasizing the slippage of language and the disintegration of knowledge as much as it does, reveals a fundamental tension in Beauvoir's work in general: the tension between her conviction that she has full epistemological control and her fear of slipping into the irrational chaos of the body and the emotions.

In this text a similar tension surfaces as the contradiction between Monique's experience of a full-blown epistemological crisis and her espousal of a crudely realist theory of knowledge. After an unusually friendly conversation with Maurice, she concludes that language cannot change anything after all. In fact, giving things different, more comfortable names makes her feel cheated:

> It was delightful talking with him, like two friends, as we used to do. Difficulties grew smaller; questions wafted away like smoke; events faded; true and false merged in an iridescence of converging shades. Fundamentally, nothing had happened. I ended up by believing that Noëllie did not exist. . . . Illusions: sleight of hand. In fact this comfortable talk has not changed anything in the very least. Things have been given other names: they have not altered in any way. I have learnt nothing. The past remains as obscure as ever; the future as uncertain. (pp. 180–1/207–8)

Caught in her own homespun version of philosophical realism, one which divorces language from reality, she concludes that language is useless, a mere surface game which never influences the underlying reality in any way. Truth and reality become one and the same thing, equally abstract and absolute: both are indestructible, outside language, outside time, fixed for all eternity: 'This love between us was real: it was solid – as indestructible as truth' (p. 195/223). While ostensibly intended to protect truth and reality from the corroding effects of doubt, Monique's epistemology, by turning her own experience of flux and uncertainty into non-knowledge, can only reinforce her suffering. Language will, for instance, be incapable of catching the very essence of what she proudly calls her 'sincerity'. This is doubly tragic, because she derives a large part of her own identity precisely from her sincerity: 'I try to say exactly what I think, what I feel; so does he; and there is nothing that seems more precious to us than this sincerity' (p. 137/158–9). But in the light of her increasing distrust of language, the 'sincerity' Monique thought she and Maurice set above all other values can be nothing but a sham: the most sincere confession of true feeling will never change 'reality'.

There should be no need to emphasize the distance between such fatalism and Beauvoir's own view of language and action. Beauvoir is, after all, the woman who as late as 1962 declared that: 'I am an intellectual. I take words and the truth to be of value' (*Force of Circumstance*, p. 378/II.120). From the author's perspective, Monique's lack of confidence in language turns out to be yet another trace of her principal crime: that of *not* being the bearer of knowledge and truth; that of not being an intellectual.

The rhetorics of identification

The readings outlined above are almost exclusively thematic: very little attention is being paid to the rhetorical strategies of the text. In the case of this particular short story, however, perhaps the single most important factor to influence the reader is a purely formal structure: the diary form, with its characteristic use of the first-person singular narrator.

As we have already seen, Beauvoir intends to turn the reader into a detective. In one way this places the reader in a position of subservience to the author of the plot: she is after all simply decoding the puzzles set by the author, following the beaten path to the inevitable end, as it were. However, this strategy also assumes that the reader in the end will have accumulated all the knowledge the author alone originally possessed. As such it seeks to turn the reader into the author's double. In this way Beauvoir's rhetorical strategy aims for a Romantic identification between reader and author: an identification where the reader knows her place. Apart from being highly flattering for the author, this kind of hierarchical symbiosis is uncannily like Monique's deluded view of her relationship with Maurice: they are one – but *he* is the one they are. Thus Beauvoir is caught in a glaring contradiction between her thematic condemnation of her protagonist and her persistent efforts to enact the very same delusions on the rhetorical level.

But if Monique's marriage fails, so does Beauvoir's rhetorical struggle. This is first and foremost an effect of Monique's first-person singular narration. Her suffering and despair come across with a quite unusual intensity which rarely fails to elicit the reader's sympathy. In the Beauvoirean scheme of things, the intensity is more likely to be caused by the author's loathing for the hapless Monique, than by any great sympathy with her plight. There is a considerable gap between Beauvoir's cold-blooded plotting of her 'detective story' and the passionate suffering which, quite against all the rules of the traditional detective thriller, she attributes to the woman she claims to have set up as the criminal. If her rhetorical strategies do not work it is because she has failed to study the formal rules of the detective story closely enough. To make the criminal hide behind the mask of a first-person singular narrator, is unusual, to say the least. When Agatha Christie tried it, in *The Murder of Roger Ackroyd*, her readers felt cheated. It is like making the counsel for the defence the murderer: it is violating the rules of the game by setting an illicit trap for the reader, and provides a far too easy way out for the author, who no longer has to construct a really clever set of 'licit' clues.

Monique's lack of knowledge makes her incapable of constructing a coherent narrative: Beauvoir makes her 'contradictions' one of the most incriminating pieces of evidence against her, accusing her, as we have seen, of 'weav[ing] the darkness in which she sinks far down', since 'from one page to another her diary contradicts itself'. These contradictions, moreover, are themselves a quagmire of ignorance, a set of 'fresh omissions and new falsehoods' (*ASD*, p. 140/175). If Peter Brooks is right in his interpretation of Freud's *Dora*, for Freud the very fact of producing an incoherent narrative is a sign of neurosis ('Psychoanalytic Constructions', p. 54). But in this sense, Brooks points out, the work of analysis and that of detection have more than one feature in common:

> [The detective story] equates the incomplete, incoherent, baffling story with crime, whereas detection is the making of an intelligible, consistent and unbroken narrative. . . . The narrative chain, with each event connected to the next by reasoned causal links, marks the victory of reason over chaos, of society over the aberrancy of crime, and restitutes a world in which aetiological histories offer the best solution to the apparently unexplainable. ('Psychoanalytic Constructions', p. 54)

One might add that the *reason* why the neurotic fails to produce coherence is that she lacks the *power* to impose her own connections on her reader/listener. Freud is very explicit about the way in which the analytic situation is a scene of *struggle*, if not in *Dora*, then in his papers on technique from 1911 to 1915. In 'Remembering, Repeating and Working Through' (1914), he sees analysis as armed combat: 'The patient brings out of the armory of the past the weapons with which he defends himself against the progress of the treatment – weapons which we must wrest from him one by one' (p. 151). In 'The Dynamics of Transference' (1912) he summarizes his findings on transference by stressing the need for *victory* for the analyst: 'This struggle between the doctor and the patient, between intellect and instinctual life, between understanding and seeking to act, is played out almost exclusively in the phenomena of transference. Victory must be won – the victory whose expression is the permanent cure of the neurosis' (p. 108). There is in 'The Woman Destroyed' more than a superficial similarity between Beauvoir's position in relation to her character, and that of Freud *vis-à-vis* Dora. In both cases, what is at stake in the narrative struggle is the right to claim one's own knowledge as truth, and, as a corollary, the right to proclaim the guilt of one's defeated opponent.

But what exactly are the effects of the first-person singular narrative? For Emile Benveniste, before it is anything else, all actual use of language is an utterance, an act of *enunciation*. The act of enunciation produces (*instaure*) the discourse as discourse. This has a series of implications. First of all, the speaker cannot fail to signal her position as speaker (*locuteur*). Secondly, the very act of signalling one's place as a speaker establishes an 'other', a 'you' to whom the utterance is addressed. Finally, the act of enunciation is already, in its very formal effects the 'expression of a certain relationship to the world' ('L'appareil formel', p. 82). This means that the enunciation always in some way or other reveals the 'attitudes of the enunciator towards that which he or she enounces' (p. 85). And one of the main aims of the enunciation is to *influence* the listener, or in other words: every act of enunciation necessarily embodies a rhetorical strategy directed towards the 'you' implied by the speaking 'I'. As Gérard Genette has shown, this is no less true for texts which ostensibly signal their impersonality by extensive use of third-person narrative, the *passé simple* and so on.[13] A monologue is no exception to this rule: it is simply a variation on the basic structure which is the dialogue. Fictional acts of enunciations are nevertheless more complex than ordinary utterances, in that they take place on at least two levels, that of the writer and that of her characters (see Benveniste, 'L'appareil formel', p. 88).

In 'The Woman Destroyed', there are two subjects of

enunciation: the implicit I of the literary act of enunciation, which produces its own dialogic I/you relation, and that of the fictional character, the I of the *énoncé*, that is, the statement produced by the enunciation. The primary rhetorical relation which is to be established here is that between the author and the reader, where the reader is to be made to respond correctly to the clues laid down by the enunciator. Beauvoir's failure is the failure properly to establish this I/you relation. Instead, the competing I of the *énoncé* takes over as the predominant speaking subject, producing the reader in *her* image. The reader then becomes involved in doubling *her* perspective, endlessly inventing excuses for her, even ending up feeling cross with Beauvoir for placing Monique in such dire straits.

What happens here might best be described as a case of double transference: positive transference on to the character, negative on to the author. Transference may among other things be characterized as a relation of identification and as a demand for love. In his 'Observations on Transference-Love' (1915), Freud argues that: 'There can be no doubt that the outbreak of a passionate demand for love [in the analytic situation] is largely the work of resistance' (p. 162). When this happens the patient 'becomes quite without insight' (p. 162), and mobilizes the strongest drive-based opposition to the intellectual work of analysis. Much the same seems to be the case when an author writes for love. In 'The Woman Destroyed', the writing subjects both write to be loved. In Monique's case this is obvious; Beauvoir's is more complex. But in the *Memoirs of a Dutiful Daughter* (1958) she explicitly presents her vocation as a writer as one inspired by the desire for love and recognition. Crying over the destiny of George Eliot's Maggie Tulliver, she stresses her identification with Maggie, and then goes on to predict her future career as a writer: 'Through the heroine, I identified myself with the author: one day other adolescents would bathe with their tears a novel in which I would tell my own story' (p. 140/195, trans. amended). The trouble in 'The Woman Destroyed' is that if the reader recognizes the demands of the author, she will have to deny her sympathy to the character: it is difficult, to say the least, at one and the same time to identify with the mature lucidity of the author, and cherish the victim of that superior intellect.

As the subject of the enunciation, Beauvoir displays a markedly negative transference on to the subject of the *énoncé*, deliberately setting out to break or destroy her. The vehemence of her rhetorical sadism, however, ends up mobilizing the reader's support for the victimized Monique. There is nevertheless nothing automatic about this process, since similar support is not forthcoming in the case of the monologue of Murielle in the short story entitled 'The Monologue' (published in the same volume as 'The Woman Destroyed'). In the case of Murielle, it is clear that she is a wholly despicable character and, from the bourgeois point of view, also an obvious failure: she is a many-times divorced wife, and mother of a daughter who committed suicide to escape her control. In the case of Monique, however, the reader is presented with the epitome of a thoroughly nice and decent upper-middle-class housewife. Beauvoir's story is a full-scale attempt to deprive the apparently successful bourgeois wife and mother of the last shreds of her claims to happiness: Monique loses her husband, her two daughters and her own identity, and is left with absolutely nothing. The total absence of self-reflexive irony, or indeed of any kind of humour, points to the same transferential lack of distance her subject matter.[14]

There is a striking parallel between Monique's experience, where what she takes to be her own identity dissolves along with every other certainty, and Marx and Engels's graphic description of the constant revision and dissolution required by the bourgeois mode of production:

> Everlasting uncertainty and agitation distinguish the bourgeois epoch from all earlier ones. All fixed, fast-frozen relations, with their train of ancient and venerable prejudices

and opinions are swept away, all new-formed ones become antiquated before they can ossify. All that is solid melts into air, all that is holy is profaned, and man is at last compelled to face with sober senses, his real conditions of life, and his relations with his kind. (*Communist Manifesto*, p. 83)

For Marx and Engels this process of disintegration is part of a larger dialectical structure, in which old illusions must be shed in order to open the way for new insights. Monique's breakdown, however, is decidedly undialectical: in this text the particular hallmark of Beauvoir's vision is the lack of *any* positive moment of reconstruction, however implicit. It is as if the text takes a perverse pleasure in slowly and deliberately blocking every issue for its protagonist, leaving her to face nothing but unlit windows and closed doors. It is in this sense that the feminists in 1968 were right to criticize the story: in the end it does not allow for change, let alone revolutionary transformation.

In 'Remembering, Repeating and Working Through', Freud writes that during the analysis, the patient 'does not listen to the precise wording of his obsessional ideas' (p. 152). In other words: to be in the grip of transference is to neglect one's rhetoric. If Beauvoir's act of enunciation fails to persuade her readers to take up the position prepared for them, it is precisely because of the way in which the identificatory logic of transference prevents her from paying sufficient attention to the metonymical strategies of rhetorical displacement.[15] In this case, what is required in order to perceive the rhetorical logic of the text is neither a reader-detective, sharing the author's transferential investment in epistemological superiority, nor a reader-victim, identifying with the plight of the protagonist, but rather a reader-analyst who, in the words of Freud, will 'maintain the same evenly-suspended

attention in the face of all that one hears' ('Recommendations', pp. 111–12). That would seem to be the only way
in which we might come to perceive the transferential play
of rhetoric and identification or, as Peter Brooks puts it,
'understand narrative as both a story and the discourse
that conveys it, seeking both to work on the text, and to
have the text work on us' ('Psychoanalytic Constructions',
p. 74).

NOTES

I am grateful to Elizabeth Fallaize and Peter Brooks for their
comments on an earlier version of this paper.

1 The English title sounds too melodramatic. 'A Broken
Woman' would perhaps be a more literal translation of 'La
femme rompue'.

2 This is not quite correct. Exceptionally among Beauvoir's
fiction, the story appeared in instalments in the popular
women's magazine *Elle* in the autumn of 1967, that is to say
a few months before it was published as the title story in a
volume of three short stories in January 1968. The volume
was a run-away bestseller on publication. But already in the
autumn of 1967, Beauvoir published the title story in a
special volume illustrated by sixteen engravings by her sister,
Hélène de Beauvoir. Beauvoir accepted serialization in *Elle*,
accompanied by her sister's engravings, in order to get more
publicity for this special edition. This somewhat complex
publication history seems to be the reason why some sources
give 1967 and some 1968 for the volume of short stories as
a whole. The two other stories, 'The Age of Discretion' and
'The Monologue', however, were not published until January
1968.

3 I am referring to Kristeva's development of the theory of the
speaking subject, and Benveniste's exploration of the act of
enunciation. The reason why I mention Kristeva at all in the
context of a paper where I only explicitly draw on Benveniste
is to draw attention to the difference between Benveniste's
transcendental ego and Kristeva's psychoanalytical speaking

subject. In general I read Benveniste through Kristeva's work.

4 All page references to works by Beauvoir are given in the text. Page numbers on their own refer to 'The Woman Destroyed', other references are preceded by an abbreviated form of the title. Although I have been working with the French texts, I give all quotations in English. However, in order to facilitate rapid consultation of the original, I also supply page references to the French editions used. The first page number refers to the English translation, the second to the French original. Full references to the editions used are given in the References. 'Trans. amended' indicates that I have changed the translation. In some cases I have not been able to consult a published translation. In such cases, or where no English translation exists, I give only one page reference, to the French text, and supply my own translation.

I have no such scruples about quotations from other sources. In general, I have tried to use published English translations, but this has not always been possible. I give my own translations wherever I rely on an original text. The one page reference supplied is always to the edition listed in the References.

5 Writing in the conservative *Figaro littéraire*, Pivot rushed into print on 30 October 1967 – that is to say, *before* the last instalments had appeared in *Elle*. It is only fair to point out that Pivot's aggression stems as much from his arrogant and sexist devaluation of 'la presse féminine' as from his dislike of Beauvoir and her well-known political positions. 'Truly, "The Woman Destroyed" is a whole women's magazine by itself', he writes. 'It is *Elle* in *Elle*. So far, only the horoscope is missing' (p. 29). Pivot's reaction, as well as that of Jacqueline Piatier, the influential critic of *Le Monde* (who, unlike Pivot, managed to wait until she had read the whole volume before reviewing it), raises the question of Beauvoir's status as a writer of popular fiction for women. The issue is far too complex to be broached here, but there can be no doubt that her best-selling status in many countries enables us to study her fiction and autobiographies from this angle. To my knowledge such a study has still to be undertaken.

6 See Buin, with contributions from Yves Berger, Jean-Pierre

Faye, Jean Ricardou, Jorge Semprun and Sartre as well as from Beauvoir.

7 See Alice Schwartzer's interview with Beauvoir, reprinted in *Simone de Beauvoir Today*.

8 There are not many full-length readings of this short story. The two most important ones are Anne Ophir's study of the whole collection of stories, and Elizabeth Fallaize's chapter on the volume in her excellent readings of Beauvoir's fiction. Mary Evans (pp. 88–90), while unaware both of the fact that her own socialist-feminist reading conflicts with the author's own, and of the unreliability of Monique as a narrator, nevertheless produces some brief, but interesting remarks towards a possible socially informed and politically transformative reading of this particular story.

9 It is nevertheless true to say that Beauvoir in no way questions such national values in this text.

10 The opposite is not necessarily true.

11 For a somewhat different study of rhetorical jealousy see my article on Andreas Capellanus's *De amore*.

12 The place visited by Monique are the famous 'Salines de Ledoux', the work of the architect Claude Nicolas Ledoux (1736–1806), constructed between 1775 and 1779, and situated in the little village of Arc-et-Senans, near Besançon. Ledoux's masterplan was to design the central salt works surrounded by concentric circles of other industrial buildings. His 'ideal city' was never used as intended, but remains one of the most monumental set of buildings of eighteenth-century France.

13 Benveniste changed his position on this point. My account is based on his 1970 paper 'L'appareil formel de l'énonciation'. But eleven years earlier, in a famous essay from 1959, 'Les relations de temps dans le verbe français', he sought to distinguish between two forms of enunciation, 'historical narrative' (*récit historique*) and discourse. The former he then defined as a mode of enunciation which excludes any 'autobiographical' trace in the language used. Prime examples were historical accounts, impersonal descriptions and so on. 'Discourse' was defined in almost exactly the same terms as those used to characterize 'enunciation' in general in 1970, that is to say as language which presupposes a 'speaker and

a listener and in the former the intention to influence the latter in any way' (p. 242). But critics such as Gérard Genette and later Jonathan Culler were quick to point out that this distinction, although certainly descriptive of different styles of language, in fact is untenable. Any utterance, however impersonally styled, necessarily intends to influence its readers/listeners. Or as Genette convincingly puts it: 'narrative exists nowhere, so to speak, in its strict form. The slightest general observation, the slightest adjective that is little more than descriptive, the most discreet comparison, the most modest "perhaps", the most inoffensive of logical articulations introduces into its web a type of speech that is alien to it, refractory as it were' (pp. 141–2). For Culler's critique of the same problem, see pp. 197–9.

14 Jacqueline Piatier, writing in *Le Monde*, deplores the lack of irony in relation to its subject matter. This point is intimately bound up with Piatier's distaste for women's magazines: 'It would have been intriguing if a story published in *Elle* actually was a parody of *Elle*', she notes.

15 The relations between transference and rhetoric have been excellently analysed by Cynthia Chase. Other aspects of literary transference are discussed by Peter Brooks in 'Narrative Transaction'. It is also necessary to point out that Freud made some important further comments on transference in his two 1937 papers, 'Constructions in Analysis' and 'Analysis Terminable and Interminable'. Infuriatingly, *none* of the important papers on transference are included in the only available paperback edition of Freud's works in Britain, the *Pelican Freud Library*, published by Penguin. Is this considered knowledge unsuitable for the so-called 'general reader'?

REFERENCES

Beauvoir, Simone de, *L'invitée* (Paris: Gallimard, 1943). Trans. Yvonne Moyse and Roger Senhouse, *She Came to Stay*, 1949 (London: Fontana, 1984).

Beauvoir, Simone de, *Pour une morale de l'ambiguïté*. Coll. idées (Paris: Gallimard, 1947). Trans. Bernard Frechtman, *The Ethics of Ambiguity* (New York: Philosophical Library, 1948).

Beauvoir, Simone de, *Le deuxième sexe* (Paris: Gallimard, 1949) 2 vols. Trans. and ed. M. H. Parshley, *The Second Sex*, 1953 (Harmondsworth, Middx.: Penguin, 1984).

Beauvoir, Simone de, *Les mandarins*, Coll. Folio, (Paris: Gallimard, 1954) 2 vols. Trans. Leonard M. Friedman, *The Mandarins*, 1957. (London: Fontana, 1986).

Beauvoir, Simone de, *Mémoires d'une jeune fille rangée*, Coll. Folio (Paris: Gallimard, 1958). Trans. James Kirkup, *Memoirs of a Dutiful Daughter* 1959 (Harmondsworth, Middx.: Penguin, 1987).

Beauvoir, Simone de, *La force de l'âge*, Coll. Folio, (Paris: Gallimard, 1960) 2 vols. Trans. Peter Green. *The Prime of Life*, 1962 (Harmondsworth, Middx.: Penguin, 1988).

Beauvoir, Simone de, 'Simone de Beauvoir', in Buin pp. 73–92.

Beauvoir, Simone de, *La Femme rompue*, Coll. Folio (Paris: Gallimard, 1968). Trans. Patrick O'Brian, *The Woman Destroyed*, 1969 (London: Fontana, 1987).

Beauvoir, Simone de, *Tout compte fait*, Coll. Folio (Paris: Gallimard, 1972). Trans. Patrick O'Brian, *All Said and Done*, 1974 (Harmondsworth, Middx.: Penguin, 1987).

Beauvoir, Simone de, 'I am a feminist', in *Simone de Beauvoir Today. Conversations 1972–1982*, with Alice Schwartzer, trans. Marianne Howarth (London: Chatto, 1984) pp. 29–48.

Benveniste, Emile, 'Les relations de temps dans le verbe français', in *Problèmes de linguistique générale, 1*, Coll. Tel. (Paris: Gallimard, 1966) pp. 237–50.

Benveniste, Emile 'L'appareil formel de l'énonciation', in *Problèmes de linguistique générale, 2*, Coll. Tel. (Paris: Gallimard, 1966) pp. 79–88.

Brooks, Peter, 'Narrative Transaction and Transference', in *Reading for the Plot. Design and Intention in Narrative* (Oxford: Clarendon Press, 1984) pp. 216–37.

Brooks, Peter, 'Psychoanalytic Constructions and Narrative Meanings', *Paragraph*, no. 7 (March 1986) pp. 53–76.

Buin, Yves (ed.), *Que peut la littérature?* Coll. L'inédit 10/18 (Paris: UGE, 1965).

Chase, Cynthia, '"Transference" as Trope and Persuasion', in *Discourse in Psychoanalysis and Literature*, ed. Shlomith Rimmon-Kenan (London: Methuen, 1987) pp. 211–32.

Culler, Jonathan, *Structuralist Poetics: Structuralism, Linguistics and the Study of Literature* (London: Routledge, 1975).

Evans, Mary, *Simone de Beauvoir: A Feminist Mandarin* (London: Tavistock, 1985).

Fallaize, Elizabeth, *The Novels of Simone de Beauvoir* (London: Croom Helm, 1988).

Freud, Sigmund, 'Recommendations to Physicians Practising Psycho-Analysis' (1912) *Standard Edition*, vol. 12, pp. 109–120.

Freud, Sigmund, 'Remembering, Repeating and Working Through' (1914) *Standard Edition*, vol. 12, pp. 146–56.

Freud, Sigmund, 'Observations on Transference-Love' (1915) *Standard Edition*, vol. 12, pp. 158–71.

Freud, Sigmund, 'Analysis Terminable and Interminable' (1937) *Standard Edition*, vol. 23, pp. 211–53.

Freud, Sigmund, 'Construction in Analysis', (1937) *Standard Edition*, vol. 23, pp. 256–69.

Genette, Gérard, 'Frontiers of Narrative', *Figures of Literary Discourse* (Oxford: Blackwell, 1982) pp. 127–44.

Kristeva, Julia, *Revolution in Poetic Language*, trans. Margaret Waller (New York: Columbia University Press, 1984).

Marx, Karl and Engels, Friedrich, *The Communist Manifesto*, 1848 (Harmondsworth, Middx.: Penguin, 1984).

Moi, Toril, 'Desire in Language: Andreas Capellanus and the Controversy of Courtly Love', in *Medieval Literature: Criticism, Ideology & History*, ed. David Aers (Brighton: Harvester, 1986) pp. 11–33.

Ophir, Anne, *Regards féminins: Beauvoir/Etcherelli/Rochefort: Condition féminine et création littéraire* (Paris: Denoël/Gonthier, 1976).

Pivot, Bernard, 'Simone de Beauvoir: Une vraie femme de lettres (pour le courrier du coeur)', *Le Figaro littéraire*, 30 October 1967, p. 29.

Piatier, Jacqueline, '"La femme rompue" de Simone de Beauvoir', *Le Monde*, 24 January 1968.

Sartre, Jean-Paul, *Lettres au Castor et à quelques autres*, ed. Simone de Beauvoir (Paris: Gallimard, 1983) 2 vols.

Sartre, Jean-Paul, *What is Literature?* trans. Bernard Frechtman, 1950 (London: Methuen, 1978).

Feminist Criticism, Theory and Politics:
An Interview with Toril Moi

PAYNE   I'd like to begin the interview with an investigation of the theory and methodology of *Sexual/Textual Politics*. Was there something in particular that encouraged you to believe that feminist literary criticism not only needed, but also could profit from the systematic critique you offer in your book?

MOI   When I was a graduate student, I wanted to do a feminist thesis on a woman writer; and I realized, this was in the late seventies, that the kind of material I was reading, which was mostly American, sometimes British, didn't say a lot about what kinds of methods and theoretical approaches would be useful and which wouldn't. Although I finished my thesis as best I could, I was deeply frustrated, because I didn't have a proper sense of what kinds of approaches, theories and methods were available to feminist critics. I couldn't find any book that talked about that, so I decided to set out to research the question better, and, in the end, to write a book on feminist literary theory. I finished the book four years later, in 1984.

Feminism, which I see as a political, or indeed revolutionary movement, is subversive and marginal to the dominant order. There's always an onus on revolutionary movements to be more self-reflective than others. We're always caught up in a struggle where we have to make decisions, where we have to try to determine our strategies, and we've got to be very much more aware than the ruling powers of what we're doing, simply in order to avoid, as far as possible, trapping ourselves in the traditional power structures. So when I set out to write a book on the theory of feminist criticism I hoped that it was going to be useful for people wanting to do feminist criticism, that it was going to be the book that I had wanted to have when I was a graduate student. I took it for granted that feminist criticism as a discipline was as good as or even better than any other forms of criticism. My book was an effort to contribute to the continuous improvement of feminist criticism. I didn't really think that it was new or unheard of to write a book that criticizes aspects of feminist strategy. That's probably got something to do with having written it in Europe. It's mostly in the United States that the point you raised has been made. I think that feminist criticism, as every other form of criticism, has some good work and some bad work in it. But I would like to stress that the texts I write about in my book are texts I consider very good, representative of the best kinds of feminist criticism. I would not bother to write about texts I found insignificant. I think that it is part of normal intellectual procedure that we sit down to reassess our theories and our thought in order to improve them. For me, the crucial thing to say about the book is that it's written from a feminist perspective, or, in other words, from a perspective of political solidarity with the feminist aims of the critics and theorists I write about. I don't think that I've solved all the problems I raise, but I certainly hope that I've stimulated further thought about them.

PAYNE Do you think that at least some of the hostile responses to your book on the one hand, and silence about the text on the other, indicate then that some people believe that your thinking is premature in, say, the history of feminist criticism?

Moi   It's a difficult question again. I think I'd like to emphasize that until the autumn of 1987 I hadn't spent a lot of time in the United States (apart from one semester spent at Cornell in 1980), so the responses you mentioned were, in a sense, not so well known to me. I've started to pick up on them now, but it wasn't something that I was very aware of. Some people probably think the book is premature, but I think others think it's already *passé*. I'm not so worried about that. The text is written entirely from the position that no statement is neutral, that a feminist piece cannot present itself as being somehow at once feminist *and* neutral, objective or universal. Accordingly I try to make my position clear throughout the book. That marking of my own position is meant to make it easier for the reader to see where my discourse is coming from. That is also to say that it makes it easier for the reader to criticize me, because the reader will not first have to detect the underlying bias through my own pretence of objectivity or neutrality. If people react critically to my book (I certainly expected that when I wrote it) I think that is partly an effect of the upfront way in which it is written. As you know, one of my points in the book is that a passive, submissive response to a text is not a response that I think feminists should encourage. So to that extent, if people are taking issue with the book or feeling that they want to have their own say after it, I can only say that, after all, I wrote it to stimulate debate, and I can't start to complain if it does so. The other part of your question was that some people react with silence, well, perhaps they do, and what can you say? You can't force everybody to talk about your book. I nevertheless feel that it is a pity if people don't want to engage with the ideas in it, *simply* because they disagree with them. If they have really felt challenged by my text, they ought to say so. I have some difficulty in understanding a deliberate effort to prevent open debate about crucial issues.

PAYNE Your introductory chapter title, 'Who's Afraid of Virginia Woolf?', and your subsequent answer to that question – 'quite a few feminist critics' – might suggest, at least to some, that you do not have complete faith or confidence in the strength of present feminist critical thinking. Does this then become paradoxical when you assume that feminist criticism is strong enough to explore itself, to seek out its own inadequacies and to attempt to rectify them?

MOI I don't see this as a contradiction. First of all, the chapter wasn't meant so much as an investigation into Virginia Woolf, as an effort to show that some of the critical attitudes we take up, as for instance when we claim that Virginia Woolf is not a good feminist, are deeply informed by the kind of theories we hold about what texts should be and how readers should be positioned in relation to them. When I picked up on Elaine Showalter's chapter on Woolf, it was not so much to show that I disagree with Showalter about Woolf, although I do, but to show *why* she arrives at her view, by pointing to the underlying theories actually informing her position. I was trying to make the point that, look, theory's important. If you don't think about theory, you aren't going to be able to see as well as you could *why* it is that you take up this rather than that position in relation to an author. You might think that your view is a natural, spontaneous response, or that it is just simply the truth. What I was trying to do, then, was to write a chapter which would 'sell' literary theory as an important subject for feminists. This is not to say, of course, that I think one ever knows one hundred per cent all the implications of one's own theory. But if one never even gives it a thought, then one has a problem. I should say that I wrote the book in a feminist environment which was extremely sceptical towards the use of theory, and so I felt that the main point of the book would be to show that *theory matters politically*. I wanted to show that one's *political* evaluations of a literary work are deeply influenced by a whole series of literary theoretical issues that one may well not even be aware of. So I was trying to say that, look, if you want to do feminist politics in literature, you've got to think about theory too.

You ask whether I have total faith in feminist criticism. If 'total faith' means that one finds no flaws and no problems, I can only say that to me that is not an intellectual stance. Is there any theory that has no room for improvement? I think that feminist criticism has come incredibly far in twenty years. It's now complicated, sophisticated, interesting and theoretically advanced. When I wrote the book in the early 1980s, things were somewhat different, and the book may already seem *passé*. I suppose it's simply a matter of saying, look, there's no finished and complete field of research, least of all feminism. I don't know any feminists who hold that feminists today have thought everything, everything we have been considering is perfect, we need to improve nothing. That's precisely what makes feminist criticism exciting! The fact that we want to keep on finding new problems and investigating weaknesses in our own procedures and so on is a sign of dynamic thought. It is not at all a matter of maturity. Right from the start, what keeps you thinking is the awareness that there's a lack in your thought, that there's something else that you need to think. The process of reflection and the process of self-reflection, or theory, if you like, go hand-in-hand right from the start. So to that extent I'd like to reject the somewhat simplistic model of a vulnerable infancy followed by robust maturity.

PAYNE   What seems to me implicit in your book, and it's made explicit toward the end of it, is the need for a redefinition of power. Is Mary Wollstonecraft's insistence that improvement in the condition of woman would occur only, and these are her words, 'if society were better organized', akin to what you see as the imperative of the reconceptualization of power, of reforming the very concept of power itself?

MOI What I took issue with was the idea that feminists should be against power, that somehow power *per se* is a bad thing, and that women should have nothing to do with it. Now I deeply disagree with that because I hold that if we don't want to have anything to do with power, then somebody else will. The question then becomes one of defining different structurations of power, different approaches to it. Just to take over power as it is now would clearly not be satisfying for us, yet I still hold that we must say that we want power because we certainly don't want the patriarchs to keep it. Feminism, among other things, is about the need to reconceptualize power, understand it differently, see the creative potential in power. Feminists have been very good at showing up the negative consequences of powerlessness. I mean we have seen the depression, the inertia, the self-deprecation that can come out of oppression, of always finding oneself in a position of powerlessness. We have perhaps not investigated the enabling aspects of power well enough. But to get back to your point about Wollstonecraft. As a socialist feminist, I certainly believe that you need to restructure society itself, and that the feminist struggle therefore cannot be defined narrowly as simply a struggle for women, if that struggle for women doesn't encompass a transformation of power structures under, say, monopoly-capitalism as well. Just as I don't think that there can ever be a socialist society which is truly socialist if it's not also feminist, I also think that feminism cannot really achieve what I take to be its utopian ideals under capitalism. So somehow or other that tricky and very difficult process of making feminism inform socialism and making socialism inform feminism would be necessary if we are to get somewhere with a new idea of power.

PAYNE With the financial, social and political power in

the hands of men, is it then necessary for there to be a revolutionary redefinition of power so that women can gain what they need, or would a fair amount of working within the system by women to attain some of their goals enable them to gain more of what they need through a change in the system from the inside?

MOI   The present situation I take to be pretty gloomy. I see the era we're in right now as one of retreat for the left, including feminism. I don't think that we can afford to be really purists about these questions. However much ideally I'd like to see feminist socialism flourish, I don't think that there is a feminist socialist revolution on the agenda for tomorrow. Today I feel that we have to work where we are, in order to change at least something. Perhaps this can help us to create a situation that may be more ripe for a deeper transformation. If we don't even do that, then we can't do anything. Then you'd end up in the kind of ultra-leftism that holds that if you can't do everything right now, you can't do a thing. So clearly I believe in working on two fronts: of course we must subvert and undermine the existing power structures from within. We're not going to be able to get completely outside them in any case, but we should have no illusions about how far such reformism will take us. Larger historical and political configurations are likely to determine whether there'll be a situation where a more profound and perhaps more rapid feminist transformation will be possible. At the moment it strikes me that it's going to be a long haul. This is a depressing insight, and it didn't look like that in the late sixties and early seventies. We'll have to work and slog on in small ways as well as in trying for the bigger ones.

PAYNE   Is there anything of a personal or existential nature in the three stages of feminism that you set forth in your text? At first glance, at least, it seems that women are to 'progress' from one stage to the next, almost like the dynamic process of coming to existential consciousness set forth in Camus's *The Myth of Sisyphus*: the awareness of a mechanical chain of daily gestures that threatens to rule the self unless there is an acceptance of that absurdity and then an affirmation of the self toward a recovery of identity. Is there something of this kind of progression in the three tiers of feminism that you describe?

MOI   First of all I wouldn't like to take credit for these three stages: I took them from Julia Kristeva's *Women's Time*. I don't think that they were ever conceived as existential or personal stages. I think they have been perceived either as moments in the women's struggle, historically and in this century, or possibly as aspects of or spaces in the women's struggle taking place today. I now see more clearly than I did when I wrote the book that it's necessary to emphasize that all the three stages must be active in our struggle at any given time. We're absolutely not in a position to transcend, say, the struggle for equal rights (stage one), and we are not in a position just to reject or to neglect the idea that women are oppressed *as women* under patriarchy, either (that would be the stage two position which emphasizes female difference). Yet I think that if we just remain in those two attitudes without a proper awareness of the constraints of having to read the world through this binary opposition of male/female all the time, we won't manage to produce a truly critical perspective on the aims of our own struggle. But there can be no question of taking up the stage three position in isolation from the two other ones. I think that Julia Kristeva herself in *Women's Time* is somewhat unclear on this point. In her text there is perhaps a tension between the claim that on the one hand these stages are always already informing each other, and on the other hand that the third position is preferable. Today I think that we must try the impossible: to keep all three going at the same time. I would now stress the necessity of making hard political choices informed by an awareness of the theoretical impossibility of doing so without substantial *loss*. Sometimes you may be in a position where different feminist lines might be taken. To choose one position is necessarily to exclude the two others. You can't possibly take up all three positions in a complex theoretical balancing act. The thing that strikes me now is that every political choice, every position, entails the loss of the others. We must be prepared to accept the *risk* of such choices, which open us up to the accusation of being wrong – and these are the consequences of your mistake. There is no way we can take up an insurance policy which will guarantee that we're in the right. I would now emphasize much more the risks of being a feminist in this contradictory space of three different positions. Such an emphasis is probably also a result of what I take to be the reactionary backlash of the eighties. Even compared to the early eighties when I wrote the book, it now seems far more difficult to be sanguine about one's feminist positions.

PAYNE   In your discussion, fairly early on in the book, of the author/madwoman, it occurred to me that this dualism might be as applicable to some male writers such as Hart Crane, whose mental illness and suicide, like Woolf's, was directly related to his art. You may recall Alvarez's *The Savage God*, where he describes what he calls extremist art, in which madness and/or suicide show the life fulfilling the destructive logic of the art.

MOI   I see this as a question both about madness and creativity, and about the relationship between authors and texts. In their pioneering book, *The Madwoman in the Attic*, Gilbert and Gubar weren't just working on an opposition of conscious author/unconscious madwoman; the interesting thing in their thesis is that it's unclear how conscious or unconscious the madwoman is; she's not necessarily an unconscious figure, but it's not clearly always a conscious strategy either, as far as I can work out from reading the book. However, the crucial point they made about the figure of the madwoman was that she was a political figure; she was a space or a location for female protest against male oppression. That's not the same thing as *any* kind of creativity or madness. All forms of creativity are not political in that specific way. So that would be the first distinction I'd like to make. I also think that Roland Barthes's aptly entitled article, 'The Death of the Author', has often been misunderstood. It is often assumed that he holds that the author no longer has any impact at all on the text, which is not the case. For Barthes in that essay the author still provides one strand in the weave of the text, one voice among the multiplicity of voices in the text. His point is that the author can no longer be the *only* source of meaning, the origin of all sense in this text. As such the author has been dethroned; I doubt that we've killed her off entirely. 'The Death of the Author' signals the death of the author as a metaphysical principle of interpretation.

It is of course important for feminists to consider very carefully the workings of the unconscious in any text. Feminist criticism has shown that it gets very far precisely with texts that represent various forms of breakdown of the symbolic ordering of traditional texts. Feminists have paid attention to those voices that seem to come from the margins, and which threaten to break up and disrupt the system. In this way any 'extremist' text, as Alvarez wants to call it, any experimental text may present an interesting challenge to further investigation for feminists. But the basic idea of the unconscious at work in language, of desire in language, is just as relevant to, say, nineteenth-century realist texts as to Crane or Plath. It's just that those texts are not deliberately trying to flaunt this desire that can never be shown but somehow hinted at. I'm very far from wanting to say that we've all got to turn to the avant-garde, whatever the avant-garde may be; I mean if I thought so I wouldn't be writing on Simone de Beauvoir at the moment.

PAYNE I should think, from your own work, that you see feminism opening up disciplines often sealed off from one another: history, philosophy, psychology, linguistics, literature, of course. Do you see this as one of the most positive elements of feminist criticism, and do you see that it makes it imperative for feminist critics to write for audiences of men as well as for audiences of women?

MOI The opening up of the interdisciplinary space that one finds in feminism is both very positive and very important. I also think that it has created some practical and political problems for feminists who are kept out of jobs, for instance, not only on the grounds that they are feminists, which we know about, but also on the grounds that, oh well, she's not really doing literary criticism is she? Isn't she more of a sociologist? But if you then apply in the sociology department, they won't touch you because they see you as more of a literature person. So there are some practical problems in that the institutions aren't always as advanced as the feminist critics are. But even outside feminism, there's been a movement within theoretically informed criticism towards greater interdisciplinarity. I have been told that religious studies are becoming very interdisciplinary, for instance. Interdisciplinarity seems to me to come with an increased awareness of the need for new theoretizations, new conceptualizations of old problems, and of course feminism would be in the forefront of wanting such new conceptualizations, but we're not the only ones.

About writing for men or women. I must admit that when I wrote *Sexual/Textual Politics*, I wrote it for other feminists, and I was obviously aware of the fact that other feminists are overwhelmingly female. I didn't have the pretension of wanting to reach, say, all women with it: it is, after all, a highly academic book. I hoped to do something towards politicizing my own discipline, but I have no illusions about the scope of that specific field. I don't think that feminist critics in general tend to transform the lives of *all* women. I felt that I was writing for other feminists, feminists interested in intellectual debates, students, postgraduate students, teachers and so on. If anybody else gets something out of the book, I would obviously be pleased, but I don't *expect* it. Writing as an intellectual today, one has a rather limited political impact, to put it mildly. But I do think that men can be feminists. But they can't be feminist in exactly the same way as women. Their role within feminism is first of all strongly to support women. If one defines feminism tentatively as a struggle against patriarchy and sexism, men clearly ought to be struggling against it as well. I think that men still have to work out what kind of voice they want to speak with in that struggle. It's certainly not a position that is easy for men to work out, and I don't think they've done enough work on it either, quite frankly. A lot of men pay lip-service to feminism, but that's as far as it goes. I would like to see them engaging actively in the struggle against patriarchy and sexism, and if they do that, I don't see why we should suspect them of not being proper feminists. So if men who want to be feminists read my book, that's fine. I think that when one writes something, one writes for a very specific group that one has in mind: that's what shapes one's rhetoric. But one clearly cannot dominate the effects of a text. What happens to it in the public space is beyond my control: it would make no sense to complain about who reads it and when and where. That's the risk you take when you publish something. Basically, then, I wrote for other feminists, and as I hold, with various modifications, that that may include men too, I'm not worried if men read it. In fact, I'm quite pleased in the sense that I feel that it is high time that men read up on feminism: they've been trying to avoid it for long enough.

I should perhaps comment briefly on what I did after

Sexual/Textual Politics. I first did *The Kristeva Reader*, which was in a sense a natural extension of my interest in Kristeva that came up with writing the first book. As an anthology it is meant to be of use to anybody who wants to study Kristeva's thought. I deliberately picked pieces from all her various phases of development: some highly controversial ones, which I would not personally say I admire a lot, and others which I see as important intellectual works. The idea was to illustrate the multiplicity of Kristeva's work and also the controversial nature of it, and then leave it to the reader to make up her own mind. For me, *The Kristeva Reader* represented an interesting task of introduction and presentation. I liked the mixture of trying to introduce these texts in a way that could make them accessible to as many people as possible, given that it is very difficult stuff, but still presenting original texts which hadn't been simplified in any way. I spent a lot of time and effort trying to make *The Kristeva Reader* into a book that people could use to start from as near scratch as possible. It was also quite challenging to have to work with the translation of highly complex theoretical texts, in collaboration with my translator, Seán Hand.

PAYNE   Let me ask you a question about that. It might be a surprise to those who read *Sexual/Textual Politics* to know that you did *The Kristeva Reader* after you did this book, because it seems to me that from the very beginning of *Sexual/Textual Politics*, you suggest that you very much agree with Kristeva's ideas, and you do use them in the book, but then in your last section, where you do go into Kristeva quite thoroughly, you appear to be highly critical of some of her views.

MOI   Readers of *Sexual/Textual Politics* will also notice that I have a great admiration for, say, *Speculum of the Other Woman*, by Luce Irigaray, which I think is an amazing book, without in any way condoning what I take to be the political and theoretical consequences of her views. If one holds that certain ideas or certain aspects of a work are extremely useful and impressive, does it really follow that one has to embrace every single line that person has ever written? Obviously such eclecticism has its dangers. One can't just pick and choose. If I say that I totally agree with Kristeva's theory of language in *Revolution in Poetic Language*, then I can't suddenly decide to leave out some obvious consequence that runs from this theory. But to my mind everything that Kristeva has written does not hold together in that way. The strength of the linguistic theory in *Revolution in Poetic Language* is not undone by the fact that Kristeva also presents it as a *social* theory of revolution which, as I say in my book, just doesn't work. I also happen to believe that the fact that the later Kristeva turns away from politics doesn't somehow retrospectively make her earlier work apolitical too. In 1974, when defending her thesis (*Revolution*), she declared that her aim was political above all. I see no reason to query that in the light of later events. It cannot ever be a matter of taking all or nothing of *any* intellectual *oeuvre*.

When I did the anthology, *French Feminist Thought*, I did it because I wanted to undermine the idea that French feminist thought consisted exclusively of Cixous, Irigaray and Julia Kristeva, which were precisely the three names I promoted in *Sexual/Textual Politics*. It struck me as quite terrible that a lot of fascinating French work in other disciplines and in the same disciplines also, within philosophy, languages and so on, should not be known to English-speaking readers. It may nevertheless be disappointing for feminists today, when we are in such a beleaguered position, to have to read, say, my work, which is all about how we have to keep on being critical towards everything all the time, even those things that we like the best. I suppose that this kind of language doesn't give anybody any kind of comfortable position from which to speak. But as you know, I speak from a fairly consistent materialist feminist position. It is just that I don't see that as a fully elaborated position at the moment. As such, at least for me, it becomes more a series of provisional positions than one, full totalization.

Both my anthologies could be said to be a detour. What I really wanted to do all along was the book on Simone de Beauvoir. As I am just about to embark on the project, it's hard for me to talk about it at the moment. One of my many starting points is that Simone de Beauvoir in many ways has been considered a dinosaur by feminists inspired by French feminist theory because she seems to believe in reason, truth, the intellect; she's been perceived as a very father-identified woman. She doesn't believe in women's language. She doesn't believe in any of the deconstructive, anti-metaphysical theories that have been so important for recent feminists, and yet she is, to my mind, the most important feminist intellectual of the twentieth century. *The Second Sex* changed thousands of women's lives, and it did so in spite of being written by a woman who declared herself not a feminist, and who only became one much later. It seems to me that there is a real need today to look at Simone de Beauvoir again, and to look at her from a position informed by all these recent theories. At the same time one must try not to fall into one or the other of the two traps that are set up for aspiring Beauvoir critics, that is, she is either idealized as the perfect feminist who could do nothing wrong; her relationship with Sartre was perfect; it was *the* example of free union; her own personal life was absolutely a model life, and she did nothing wrong in her writing and everything was wonderful. The other line is that Simone de Beauvoir betrayed her feminism all along; in fact we now know that her relationship with Sartre was morally suspect and politically more than dubious; she put other women down; she didn't really feel solidarity with women; *The Second Sex* is not at all pro-feminist; it really is a sort of exercise in traditional patriarchal philosophical arrogance and so on and so on. It is interesting in itself that there are such widely opposing views of Beauvoir. I expect that none of them is quite right. Today, because we are a bit further removed in time, it strikes me as interesting to try to do a rereading of her with present-day theoretical and political concerns in mind. It is too early for me to say exactly what I intend to do. One thing is nevertheless certain: it is the problem of the *intellectual woman* – her speaking position, her concerns, her conflicts, her intellectual styles – which fascinates me.

In this volume there will be one reading of a short story by Beauvoir, which picks up on some of the things I am interested in right now: the whole idea of knowledge, the power of knowledge, the passion for knowledge, the disasters that happen if you lose knowledge, if you have to succumb to ignorance and so on. Beauvoir is always preoccupied with the problems of knowing: knowing oneself, the other and the world. It seems to me that's where her passionate investment is. And obviously I'm also interested in the conceptualization of knowledge in Beauvoir. Is it true that it's clearly phallic and only that? Is Sartre knowledge for Beauvoir? And is she then submitting to it, or is something else going on? There are lots of interesting questions, but it's hard to talk about them at such an early stage.

Toril Moi: A Bibliography, 1978–1989

1978

1 (With Rakel Christina Granaas), 'Et annet språk – noen teoretiske innvendinger' ('A New Language – Some Theoretical Problems'), *Kontrast*, no. 3 and 4, pp. 98–100.

1979

2 'Om teori i kvinnelitteraturforskninga' ('On Feminist Literary Theory'), *Kritikk-takk*, no. 1, pp. 4–10.

3 'Kort innføring i Greimas' strukturanalyse' ('A Short Introduction to Greimasian Structural Analysis'), *Kritikk-takk*, no. 1, pp. 19–31.

4 'Greimas i praksis. Strukturer i en ukebladnovelle' ('Practical Use of Greimas: Structures in a Short Story from a Women's Magazine'), *Kritikk-takk*, no. 1, pp. 32–8.

5 'En kritisk lesning av *Adolphe*' ('A Critical Approach to *Adolphe*'), *Kritikk-takk*, no. 1, pp. 75–95.

6 'Barn–vår tids slaver' (presentation of Christiane Rochefort, *Les Enfants d'abord*), *Bergens Tidende*, 21 April, p. 5.

7 'Overdådig fryseaktivitet i Edinburgh' ('The Edinburgh Fringe'), *Bergens Tidende*, 17 September, p. 36.

1980

8 'Kvinnenatur og kvinnespråk i Frankrike' ('Female Nature and Female Language in France'), *Vinduet*, no. 3, pp. 40–1.

1981

9 (Trans.), *Female Friends* by Fay Weldon (translated as *Venninner*, Oslo: Gyldendal) 271 pp.

10 'Kvinne, språk og frigjøring. Marie Cardinals roman *Les mots pour le dire* sett i relasjon til nyere fransk kvinnelitteratur' ('Women, Language, Liberation: Marie Cardinal's *Les Mots pour le dire* in Relation to Recent Literature by Women in France'), *Edda*, no. 1, pp. 47–58.

11 'Litteraturforskning og politikk. Om det teoretiske grunnlaget for kvinnelitteraturforskninga' ('Literature and Politics. On Theory in Feminist Literary Criticism'), *Kontrast*, no. 6, pp. 44–51.

12 'Den kvinnelige utopi' ('Women's Utopia'), *Vinduet*, no. 2, pp. 32–8.

13 'Representation of Patriarchy: Sexuality and Epistemology in Freud's *Dora*', *Feminist Review*, no. 9, pp. 60–74. Reprinted in *Eigenproduksjon* (Bergen: Department of Nordic Studies), no. 18 (1983) pp. 62–76; in Bernheimer, Charles and Kahane, Claire (eds), *In Dora's Case: Feminism – Psychoanalysis – Hysteria* (New York: Columbia University Press; London: Virago, 1985) pp. 181–99; and in Spurling, Laurence (ed.), *Sigmund Freud: Critical Assessments*, vol. II (London: Croom Helm) pp. 181–95.

14 Review of Hans Jørgen Nielsen, *Fotballengelen*, *Kontrast*, no. 3, pp. 61–2.

15 Review of Lisa Alther, *Arvesynder* (*Original Sins*) and Marge Piercy, *Kvinne ved tidens rand* (*Woman on the Edge of Time*), *Samtidslitteratur 1981*, pp. 6–7.

16 Review of three Norwegian collections of short stories: *Norske Noveller 1981*, *Noveller i Samtiden*, *Så stor du er blitt*, *Samtidslitteratur 1981*, pp. 93–4.

17 Review of Birgitta Holm, *Fredrika Bremer och den borgerliga romanens födelse*, *Romanens mödrar*, 1, *Kontrast*, no. 7 and 8, pp. 79–80.

1982

18 (Trans.), *Praxis* by Fay Weldon (Oslo: Gyldendal) 267 pp. Also published in a bookclub edition the same year.

19 (Trans.), *Black Tickets* by Jayne Anne Phillips (translated as *Svarte billetter*) (Oslo: Pax) 197 pp.

20 (Trans.), *July's People* by Nadine Gordimer (translated as *Julis folk*, Oslo: Gyldendal) 165 pp. Also published in a revised bookclub edition in 1984.

21 (Trans.), *The Magic Toyshop* by Angela Carter (translated as *Den forheksede leketøysbutikken*, Oslo: Gyldendal) 205 pp.

22 (Trans.), 'Reminiscences to a Daughter', a short story by Jayne Anne Phillips (translated as 'En datters erindringer'), *Vinduet*, no. 4, pp. 25–33.

23 'Jealousy and Sexual Difference', *Feminist Review*, vol. 11 (Summer) pp. 53–68. Reprinted in *Sexuality: Essays from Feminist Review* (London: Virago) pp. 134–53.

24 'Myten om den myke mann og den store kjærlighetten: Ketil Bjørnstad's *Vinterbyen*' ('Mythical Men and Mythical Love: Ketil Bjørnstad's *Vinterbyen*'), *Vinduet*, no. 1, pp. 57–63.

25 'Psychoanalytic Approaches to Sartre's *Les Mots*', in *The State of Literary Theory Today. Proceedings from the International Association for Philosophy and Literature* (Middlesex: Middlesex Polytechnic) pp. 52–64.

26 Review of Thomas Bredsdorff, *Tristans børn. Angående digtning om kærlighed og ægteskab i den borgerlige epoke*, *Edda*, no. 4, pp. 257–60.

1983

27 (Trans.), *Puffball* by Fay Weldon (translated as *Røyksopp*, Oslo: Gyldendal) 270 pp. Also published in a bookclub edition in 1985.

28 'Musen og moren: En sammenligning av Mallarmés "Apparition" og Desnos' "Coeur en bouche"' ('Muse and Mother: A comparison of Mallarmé's "Apparition" and Desnos' "Coeur en bouche"'), *Edda*, no. 1, pp. 13–18.

29 'The Missing Mother: René Girard's Oedipal Rivalries',

Diacritics, vol. 12, no. 2 (Summer) pp. 21–31.

30 'Narcissisme som forsvar: Ibsen's *Hedda Gabler*' ('Narcissism as Defence: Ibsen's *Hedda Gabler*'), *Eigenproduksjon*, no. 18, pp. 43–61.
31 'Sexual/Textual Politics', in Barker, Francis et al. (eds), *The Politics of Theory: Proceedings of the Essex Conference on the Sociology of Literature, July 1982* (University of Essex: Colchester) pp. 1–14.
32 Review of Karin Moe, *39 Fyk*, *Kritikkjournalen*, pp. 6–7.

1984

33 'The Case of Dora' and 'Feminist Readings of Dora' in Appignanesi, Lisa (ed.), *Desire*, ICA Documents, pp. 3 and 16–17.
34 'Pornografi og fantasi: om kvinner, klær og filosofi' ('Pornography and Imagination: About Women, Clothes and Philosophy'), interview with Angela Carter, *Vinduet*, no. 4, pp. 17–21.

1985

35 *Sexual/Textual Politics: Feminist Literary Theory* (London and New York: Methuen, 'New Accents'), xviii, 206 pp.
36 'Who's Afraid of Virginia Woolf? Feminist Readings of Woolf', *Canadian Journal of Political and Social Theory*, vol. 9, no. 1–2 (Winter–Spring), pp. 133–47.
37 'Kvinnetekst, kvinnespråk, kvinneteori: Monique Wittigs *Les Guérillères*' ('Women's Text, Women's Language, Women's Theory: Monique Wittig's Novel *Les Guérillères*'), *Tribune* (Bergen), pp. 2–28.
38 'Fra skogen til skrivepulten eller faren ved den kvinnelige kreativitet: En lesning av Bjørg Vik's novelle "På bussen er det fint"') ('That Dangerous Female Creativity: Bjørg Vik's short story "It's Nice on the Bus"'), in Engelstad, Irene (ed.), *Litteratur og psykoanalyse* (Oslo: Pax) pp. 127–49.
39 'Power, Sex and Subjectivity: Feminist Reflections on Fou-

cault', *Paragraph. The Journal of the Modern Critical Theory Group*, vol. 5, pp. 95–102.

40 'Hva er kvinneforskning? Noen synspunkter til en debatt' ('What Is Feminist Research? Some Points Toward a Debate'), *Replikk*, no. 1, (November) pp. 5–9.

41 Review of Arild Kolstad, *Inga Olsens vei mot velstand og lykke, Kjerringråd*, no. 42, pp. 62–4.

42 Review of Mari Osmundsen, *Gode gjerninger, Kjerringråd*, no. 40/41, pp. 88–9.

43 Review of Rakel Christina Granaas et al. (eds), *Kvinnesyn, tvisyn* (a collection of essays on Sigrid Undset), *Kjerringråd*, no. 44, pp. 36–7.

44 Review of Elin Brodin, *Den krydrede vin, Kritikkjournalen.*

1986

45 (Ed.), *The Kristeva Reader* (Oxford: Blackwell; New York: Columbia University Press) viii, 327 pp.

46 'Desire in Language: Andreas Capellanus and the Controversy of Courtly Love', in Aers, David (ed.), *Medieval Literature: Criticism, Ideology & History* (Brighton: Harvester) pp. 11–33.

47 'Existentialism and Feminism: The Rhetoric of Biology in *The Second Sex*', in *Sexual Difference*, Special Issue of *The Oxford Literary Review*, June, pp. 88–95. Reprinted in *Arbeidsnotat 2/87* ('Kjønn og makt: teoretiske perspektiver', Oslo: NAVFs sekretariat for kvinneforskning og kvinner i forskning, 1987) pp. 83–90.

48 'Feminist Literary Criticism' in Jefferson, Ann and Robey, David (eds), *Modern Literary Theory*, 2nd edn (London: Batsford) pp. 204–21. An edited version reprinted in Belsey, Catherine and Moore, Jane (eds), *The Feminist Reader: Essays in Gender and the Politics of Literary Criticism.* (London: Macmillan; New York: Macmillan, 1989), pp. 115–32.

49 'Hele verden en scene: Karen Blixen's novelle "Storme"' ('All the World's a Stage: Karen Blixen's Short Story "Tempests"'), *Edda*, no. 2, pp. 149–61. Reprinted in Syberg, Karen (ed.), *Essays on Karen Blixen* (Copenhagen: Tiderne Skifter, forthcoming).

50 'Psykoanalyse, subjektivitet og politikk: Julia Kristeva – en

innføring' ('Psychoanalysis, Subjectivity and Politics: An Introduction to Julia Kristeva'), *Norsk Litterær Årbok* (Oslo: Det norske samlaget) pp. 151–68.

51 'Feminisme, litteraturteori og litterær analyse: Et svar til mine opponenter' ('Feminism, Literary Theory and Literary Criticism: A Reply to my Opponents'), *Edda*, no. 4, pp. 315–33.

52 'Fra kvinnelitteraturforskning til feministisk litteraturteori' ('From Women's Literature to Feminist Literary Theory'), *Nytt om kvinneforskning*, no. 1, pp. 12–17.

53 'Vive la Différence' ('The French Scene'), *The Women's Review*, March, pp. 30–1.

54 'She Came to Stay', review of Mary Evans's *Simone de Beauvoir: A Feminist Mandarin* and Judith Okely's *Simone de Beauvoir*, *Paragraph*, vol. 8, pp. 110–20.

55 'Simone de Beauvoir: In Memoriam', *Modern and Contemporary France*, vol. 27 (September) pp. 26–7.

56 'What does Carmen Want? The Enigma of *Carmen*', Programme Note for the English National Opera at the London Coliseum 1986–7, unnumbered pages. Reprinted in *The Twelfth Season, Opera Theatre of Saint Louis* (1987) pp. 50 and 78.

57 'Feminine Textuality: A View of Hélène Cixous' (Review of Verena Conley, *Hélène Cixous: Writing the Feminine*), *Quinquereme: New Studies in Modern Languages* vol. 9, no. 1, pp. 80–3.

58 Review of Mark Cousins and Athar Hussain, *Michel Foucault*, *French Studies*, vol. 60, no. 1, p. 113.

59 Review of Andrew Martin, *The Knowledge of Ignorance*, *French Studies*, vol. 60, no. 2, pp. 246–7.

60 Review of Anne-Catherine Andersen, Gerd Bjørhovde, Åse Hiorth Lervik (eds), *Oppbrudd, Skrivende kvinner over hele verden*, *Edda*, no. 3, pp. 93–4.

61 Review of Hélène Cixous, *Angst*, *The Women's Review*, January, pp. 40–1.

1987

62 (Ed.), *French Feminist Thought* (Oxford and New York: Blackwell) x, 260 pp.

63 'Kjønn og makt: teoretiske perspektiver' ('Sex and Power: On Theory'), *Nytt om kvinneforskning*, no. 2, pp. 4–6.

64 'Amtmanninnens datter' (Review article on E. Møller Jensen, *Emancipation som lidenskab: Camilla Colletts liv og værk*), *Edda*, no. 2, pp. 182–5.

65 'Depresjonens svarte sol: Julia Kristevas nyeste bok' ('The Black Sun of Depression: Julia Kristeva's New book'), *Vinduet*, no. 4, pp. 25–30. (Review article on Julia Kristeva, *Soleil noir: dépression et mélancholie*.)

66 Review of Julia Kristeva, *Revolution in Poetic Language*, *French Studies*, vol. 61, no. 1, p. 112.

67 Review of David Kelley and Isabelle Llasera (eds), *Cross-References. Modern French Theory and the Practice of Criticism*, *French Studies*, vol. 61, no. 3, p. 224.

68 Review of M. C. Weitz, *Femmes: Recent Writings on French Women* and E. D. Gelfand and V. T. Hules, *French Feminist Criticism: Women, Language and Literature. An Annotated Bibiliography*, *French Studies*, vol. 61, no. 1, pp. 114–16.

69 Review of Claire Duchen, *Feminism in France. From May '68 to Mitterand*, *French Studies*, vol 61, no. 4, p. 494.

70 Review of Malcolm Bowie, *Freud, Proust and Lacan. Theory as Fiction*, *French Studies*, vol. 61, no. 4, pp. 469–70.

71 'Pornografi' ('Pornography'), *Bergens Tidende* 18 June, p. 52.

1988

72 'Feminism, Postmodernism and Style: Recent Feminist Criticism in the US', *Cultural Critique*, no. 9 (Spring) pp. 3–22.

73 'Från text till historia: samtal med Toril Moi om litteratur och könspolitik' ('From Text to History: Conversation with Toril Moi about Literature and Sexual Politics'), interview with Sara Danius, *Bonniers Litterära Magasin* (Stockholm), vol. 57, no. 4 (September) pp. 258–64.

74 'Simone de Beauvoir – politiken och den intellektuella kvinnan' ('Simone de Beauvoir – Politics and the Intellectual Woman'), *Kvinnovetenskaplig tidskrift* (Stockholm), no. 4, pp. 3–14.

75 Review of Hélène Vivienne Wenzel (ed.), *Simone de Beauvoir:*

Witness to a Century, French Studies, vol. 62, no. 1, p. 118.
76 Review of Leo Bersani, *The Freudian Body*, *The History of the Human Sciences*, vol. 1, no. 2 (October), pp. 276–9.
77 Review of Odd Martin Mœland (ed.), *Mellom tekst og tekst. Intertekstuelle lesninger*, *Edda*, no. 4, pp. 363–5.
78 'The Truth of Feminism', *Edda*, no. 4, pp. 361–2.
79 Review of Nicole Ward Jouve, *Colette, Modern and Contemporary France*.

1989

80 'Men Against Patriarchy', in Linda Kauffmann (ed.), *Gender and Theory: Dialogues on Feminist Criticism* (Oxford and New York: Blackwell) pp. 181–8.
81 'Patriarchal Thought and the Drive for Knowledge', in Teresa Brennan (ed.), *Between Feminism and Psychoanalysis* (London and New York: Routledge), pp. 189–205.
82 '1949/Simone de Beauvoir: An Intellectual Woman in Postwar France', in Denis Hollier (ed.), *The Harvard History of French Literature* (forthcoming).
83 '"I Desire the Law": *La Traviata* or the Misguided Daughter', Programme Note for the English National Opera.
84 '"She Died Because She Came Too Late . . .": Knowledge, Doubles and Death in Thanas's *Tristan*', *Exemplaria* (forthcoming).
85 Review of Barbara Johnson, *A World of Difference*, *SubStance*, no. 59 (forthcoming).
86 Review of Shlomith Rimmon-Kenan (ed.), *Discourse in Psychoanalysis and Literature. Free Associations*, no. 17 (forthcoming).
87 'Moa Martinsson as Modernist', review of Ebba Witt-Brattström, *Moa Martinsson – skrift och drift i trettiotalet*, *Kvinnovetenskaplig tidsskrift* (Stockholm), no. 1, pp. 70–4.
88 Review of Michel Foucault, *Politics, Philosophy, Culture: Interviews and Other Writings 1977–1984*, ed. Lawrence D. Kritzman, *French Studies* (forthcoming).
89 Review of Ruth Sherry, *Studying Women's Writing*, *Edda*, (forthcoming).

Index